# FREEDOM OF THE INDIVIDUAL

# FREEDOM OF THE INDIVIDUAL

### Stuart Hampshire

*Warden of Wadham College, Oxford
and formerly Professor of Philosophy,
Princeton University*

EXPANDED EDITION

1975

PRINCETON UNIVERSITY PRESS
PRINCETON, NEW JERSEY

First published by Chatto and Windus Ltd.,
London, in association with the University
of Otago Press, Dunedin, New Zealand, 1965

Expanded Edition, 1975, published by
Princeton University Press

ISBN: 0-691-07208-6 (Hardcover)
ISBN: 0-691-01984-3 (Princeton Paperback edition)

Printed in the United States of America
by Princeton University Press, Princeton, New Jersey

*To my wife*

# CONTENTS

Preface                              *page*  9

*Chapter*
1  Two Kinds of Possibility             11

2  Desire                               34

3  Two Kinds of Knowledge               53

4  Conclusion                          104

5  Determinism and Psychological
   Explanation: a Postcript            113

# PREFACE TO THE SECOND EDITION

This essay is an extended version of the De Carle Lectures delivered at the University of Otago at Dunedin, New Zealand, in July and August 1964, and it was published in accordance with the requirements of that lectureship. I am deeply grateful to the University of Otago for the opportunity offered to me, and for the hospitality and encouragement that I received in Dunedin. I only wish that I had been able to treat the issues, within the span of these lectures, with a thoroughness appropriate to the issues, and with a clarity appropriate to the occasion.

I am especially grateful to Professor Daniel Taylor, and to members of the Department of Philosophy at the University of Otago, for many stimulating discussions during my stay there, and for their criticisms. I am grateful also to the University of Otago Press, co-publishers of the first edition, for its helpfulness. Professor George Pitcher, of Princeton University, read the original manuscript, and, without his suggestions, it would have been even more inadequate than it is. I am very grateful to the Guggenheim Foundation for a Fellowship which gave me the time to develop some of the arguments mentioned in Chapter 5, which I have added as a postscript.

JULY 1974                                                      S.H.

*Chapter 1*

# TWO KINDS OF POSSIBILITY

I first consider two pairs of propositions: their implications, and the kind of observation and argument by which their truth or their falsity would normally be established, if they were challenged.

*The first pair*
(a1) 'It will not happen now'
(a2) 'It cannot happen now'

*The second pair*
(b1) 'He will not do it now'
(b2) 'He cannot do it now'

To bring out the contrast between the pairs, one might choose more specific propositions as examples of the two types:

(A1) 'The gas will not escape now'
(A2) 'The gas cannot escape now'
(B1) 'Jones will not escape now'
(B2) 'Jones cannot escape now'

I am concerned with the difference between 'will not' and the 'cannot' in the two cases: I shall argue that it is a different difference.

Consider the first pair first: to make the transition from 'It will not happen now' to 'It cannot happen now,' from the weaker to the stronger statement, is, at the very least, to claim that a certain type of evidence, or reason for believing, or source of knowledge, that the thing will not happen is available: not only will it not happen, but it is impossible that it should. Someone might agree that the thing won't happen,

11

but he might at the same time dispute the stronger statement that it cannot happen, that it is impossible that it should. 'I agree with you,' he says, 'that in fact it will not happen now; but, all the same, it might; it is not altogether impossible. Your statement is too strong.'

We see that the contradictory of 'It cannot happen here and now' is not only 'It can, or could, happen here and now,' but also 'It may, or it might, happen here.' These are alternative ways of representing the possibility of its happening, when someone has asserted the impossibility. When the two disputants agree about the future course of events—that in fact the thing will not happen—they may still disagree about the possibility of its happening. If it is certain that it will not happen, there is no possibility that it will.

I do not myself know of any entirely adequate account of the logic of statements of the form 'It is certain that so-and-so will not happen.' But at least it is clear that he who asserts that it is certain that it will not happen here, or alternatively asserts that it cannot happen here, must show that there are very strong grounds for believing, or that there is some sure source of knowledge, that it will not happen here, when the truth of his statement is challenged. A man may say 'It will not happen here,' (e.g. 'This horse will not win the race'), and his statement may be true, and the utterance may be an entirely justifiable utterance in the circumstances, even though he was not in a position to support the statement with good grounds, or good evidence, or by citing a source of knowledge. But 'It cannot happen here,' which denies that it might happen, asserts, at the very least, that there are very good reasons for believing that it won't. Perhaps it is sometimes, or even generally, used to assert, or imply, much more than this: e.g. that there is some well-established natural law covering this happening; perhaps it asserts, or implies, that there is some cause, or sufficient condition, of its not happening. However this may be, at least it asserts that there are grounds for believing that it will not happen, which are strong enough to justify the assertion that it cannot happen. If no such grounds exist, the statement 'It can't happen here' is unsustainable and incorrect, even if the statement 'It won't happen here' is acceptable; for an objector could say 'Well, I admit that it didn't happen: but still it might have happened, and you were quite wrong when you said that it couldn't happen.'

We are familiar with the series: (1) 'It might happen here,' which might also be expressed as 'It could happen here;' (2) 'It is unlikely to happen here,' but 'It might' or 'It could,' and (3) 'It is certain that it won't happen here,' which might be expressed as 'It can't.'

Turn now to the second pair of the original propositions: either to the more general 'He won't do it now' and 'He can't do it now': or to the more specific 'He won't escape' and 'He can't escape.' The transition from 'He won't' to 'He can't' may here be altogether different; for when we say that he can't do it, we are not ordinarily saying that it can't be the case that he will do it. Given an appropriate verb of action, we would not ordinarily be denying that he might do it, that there is a possibility that he will. We are rather saying that he is not able to do it, that he lacks the means, or the authority, or the opportunity, to do it. The transition from 'He won't escape now' to 'He can't escape now' would not ordinarily be a transition from a weaker to a stronger statement about a future happening—about a possible eventuality, his escape. The conjunction of 'can' with a verb representing voluntary action would ordinarily preclude this interpretation; only in the past tense 'He can't have escaped' would ordinarily have as its contradictory 'He might have escaped,' where this is equivalent to 'It is not impossible that he did.' 'He could have escaped,' is ambiguous when taken out of context. It might be intended to be equivalent to 'It could be the case that he escaped', and 'It is not impossible that he did,' and 'He might

13

have escaped;' or it might be intended to be equivalent to 'He had the ability, the means, and the opportunity, to escape.'

'He can't escape' may be informative as giving a reason or explanation why in fact he won't. He won't escape, because he can't. It is informative as a reason or explanation, because it may be the case that he would escape if he could, but he can't. Contrast this with the other pair: of the gas it is not similarly informative to explain the fact that it won't escape now by saying that it can't. It is not clear what it would mean to say of a gas that it would escape if it could. It is just conceivable that some non-anthropomorphic, literal sense might be given to this; for example, that it is a gas which has a tendency to escape from any container, but that now its escape is obstructed. But 'It would, if it could, but it can't' is not a literal and natural, and even less a scientific way, of speaking of the behaviour of a gas; more natural would be 'It would escape if it wasn't for the lead in the container, which makes it impossible.' Here 'It's impossible' does not actually give the reason why it won't escape; it indicates only that there is a specific cause of its not escaping, in spite of its tendency to escape. If I am asked to give you a reason for believing that it won't escape, I may explain to you why it can't. But I cannot quote its inability to escape as a reason for its not escaping. On the other hand, 'He would if he could, but he can't' is a very natural, and informative, way of speaking of the behaviour of a person. We now know in very general terms why he won't escape: he lacks the ability, or the means, or the opportunity to escape.

'He can't do it' (the governor is speaking about the prospect of his escape from prison) gives one of two possible reasons or explanations of why he won't. The other is that he does not want to do it, or is unwilling to do it; for, if he doesn't do it, it is generally either *vouloir* or *pouvoir*, the will or the power, that is lacking. If both were present, and present in full measure and without qualification, that is, if no other desire were more urgent, he generally would do it. I add the qualification 'generally,' because there is a third possible explanation, which may perhaps not be accounted for as a special case of having a conflicting desire: the explanation given in the words 'because he thinks he ought not to escape.' 'Because he doesn't want to,' or 'because he wants something else more,' explains his not doing it, in the same way that 'He can't do it' explains. It excludes one of two obvious possibilities, and therefore it tells one more about the situation. To the gas, and to inanimate things generally, the concept of wanting neither has, nor can be given, any application. Consequently, 'The gas cannot escape now,' taken by itself, is no kind of explanation of its not escaping. For it does not exclude one of these two possibilities.

The statement 'He cannot escape now' of course has as its contradiction 'He can.' 'He can escape' does not entail 'He might escape.' For it might be the case that, although he is able to escape, there is no possibility that he will want to. Nor does 'He might escape' entail 'He can escape.' 'He might escape' only entails 'He might be able to escape,' but not the unmodified statement that he can. Of course 'He cannot' does entail 'He will not,' but it does not entail 'It is certain that he won't,' or 'There is no possibility that he will,' both of which are contradicted by 'He might.' He cannot escape now, at this moment' is an unmodified, categorical statement about him, on a level with the categorical statement 'He is unwilling to.' He lacks the power now, at this moment. The question may be asked 'Is it certain that he cannot?' or 'Is it possible (might it be) that he can?' There is nothing odd in the question 'Can it be (i.e., is it possible) that he cannot escape?' That the two kinds of 'can' should occur in the same sentence may be disagreeable in style; but the sense is not unclear. It may be possible or impossible that he can escape, just as it may be possible or impossible that he actually will. It may be certain that he lacks the ability; and we may

15

be in a position to point to some necessary condition of his having the ability which is lacking.

Just as we might in some cases seek for scientific explanation of a man's doing something, we look also for causal explanations of his power, or of his lacking the power, to do something. 'Why was I unable at that moment to do so-and-so?' is typically a causal question; my powers to do certain things come and go, are present at one moment and not at another, and I have every motive for discovering, if I can, the conditions on which their presence and their absence depend. Sometimes, of course—as, typically, in the case of escaping—the answer to the question 'Why can't he?' may be entirely obvious, and no experiment, or careful causal investigation, may be needed. It is often obvious that it is impossible, and out of the question, that a man should be able to do something, just as it is often obviously impossible, and out of the question, that he will want to do something. We may always look for sufficient conditions of the existence, or non-existence, of a power to do certain things. We need to acquire, and to hold on to, abilities, and we therefore need to know the conditions on which their existence depends.

There are some things which I can do at one moment and cannot do at the next; in this sense, powers can be very episodic, and impotence the matter of a moment. 'Why can't I do it now? I could do it a moment ago.' At one moment I can remember something that I want to remember: at the next moment I cannot. Evidently, there are also powers which, once acquired, last all one's life, and there are others that are intermediate between these two extremes. There are powers that are in their nature intermittent, and also powers that are not specific—e.g. the ability to speak French: just as there are desires and inclinations and interests that are in their nature intermittent, and also those that are not specific. I wish to concentrate on the power to do a specific thing on a particular occasion, because this is the fundamental kind of power, and of potentiality, which philosophers have tended to neglect, particularly in the context of an individual's freedom of decision.

You may now ask—What is a power, as this is attributed to human beings? How is it identified, and how is its existence or non-existence recognized? Is there a sharp line between powers to do something, attributed to human beings, and the causal properties of physical things, e.g. machines? I think there is: perhaps not a sharp line, but a line.

I have so far only said that the concept of a power to do some specific thing is complementary to the notion of a will, or of wanting to do something: associated with the concept of an action, the *vouloir* and *pouvoir*, 'want' and 'can', depend on each other for their sense. Whether someone lacks the power to do something is tested in actual performance, but only subject to the condition that the subject had the will to do the thing in question: whether someone lacks the will to do something may sometimes be revealed (in part, and only in part, and the lack is not conclusively established) in actual performance, but only subject to the condition that the power to do the thing in question exists. To speak of a man wanting to do a particular thing on a particular occasion (e.g. having the urge to speak, or to protest) is not to speak of a tendency, in that sense of 'tendency' in which a gas may have a tendency to escape, as some philosophers have suggested. A human desire or inclination to do something is not only, or primarily, revealed in actual performance, as is the tendency of a gas. I normally discover, decide, and know what I want to do, quite independently of observing my own patterns of behaviour; and I may authoritatively, though not infallibly, disclose my desires and interests to others, together with the conceptions and calculations that enter into them. It may be true that I did have an impulse to protest, even though no evidence of this is to be found in my behaviour, and even though no test would establish that I did, or did not, have at that moment that impulse; for to ask me about my impulse is not to apply a test, in the sense in which you may apply a test to establish that this particular gas has a tendency to escape at this particular time. For these reasons—or connected with these facts—a statement to the effect that someone—say, the speaker —wants, or wanted, to do something at a particular moment is not equivalent to any set of hypothetical statements about his observable behaviour. A desire to act may occur at a particular moment, and may be no less an episode in a man's biography, to be reported in a categorical statement, than a twinge of pain, or a blow on the head. A desire, or inclination, to do something at a particular moment does not need to be tested in performance—or to be tested at all—unlike a power to do something, which does in the last resort need to be tested in performance, if its existence is to be established beyond doubt.

Compare (a) 'At that moment I wanted to race him and overtake him but, of course, I didn't;' (b) 'At that moment I could have overtaken him, but, of course, I didn't.'

The first statement may in normal circumstances be known to be true, beyond doubt, and quite independently of the inductive test of parallel cases; in such a simple case the first person disclosure is authoritative, although not immune from various kinds of error, from self-deceit, or deceit. The question 'How do you know that you wanted to?', as opposed to 'Are you sure?', is normally senseless. In the second case, the inductive test of parallel cases is the relevant test, and the first person statement is not authoritative. The question 'How do you know that you could have' is far from senseless. Whether I have, or had, the power to overtake, as I believe, only experience and experiment can show. Whether I have, or had, the desire is not normally, and in the standard case, to be finally settled by experience and experiment. In the normal case the subject, although liable to correction, can claim to know directly what he wants to do. There can be no question of the source of his knowledge; it is direct knowledge, in the sense that it has no source.

The notion of a power, as expressed in the form 'I can do so-and-so,' 'He can do so-and-so,' is a very wide and general one. It includes the kind of power to do something which is an ability or skill, the power which is being in a position to do something, either in a literal or a metaphorical sense, a legal or customary power to do something (e.g. to marry people, if I am a priest), and many variations and combinations of these. Whenever, in respect of any action, the contrast between the attempt to do and the achievement is in place, the notion of the power to do it is also in place. Plainly the question 'Can you do it?' will sometimes be an absurd question; either the verb of action in itself, or the circumstances of the particular case, may show that the question does not arise. But, in general, it is intrinsic to the notion of an action that it is something that can be attempted, and attempted successfully, that it is something that one may try to do, and that one may either succeed in doing or fail.

I may seem to be leaning rather heavily at this point on the unanalysed, and probably unanalysable, notion of a verb of action. By what criteria are we to distinguish a verb which represents a person's action, in the required sense, from among all the verbs applicable to persons? Is it not notorious that this cannot be done? And yet am I not assuming, in my account of a power to do something, as being distinct from a causal property, that we can distinguish the cases of 'He can X,' where X is a verb, which are cases of the power to *do* something, in some strong sense of 'do,' from cases where 'do' is used with some weaker sense? (a) The doctor says 'He cannot live through the night.' (b) The prison governor says 'He cannot escape.' Is 'live' in this context a verb of action in the required sense? It is not. A man lives through the night only as the vegetative soul dictates, and as a vegetable does; his choosing to live or die cannot here be at issue, as his choice

19

might be at issue in estimating whether he will escape. Must one therefore distinguish two different uses of 'can' in these sentences? I am suggesting that, at least for some purposes, one must. I say to a particular man that he can today continue to climb the mountain, amidst the snow and ice, when such-and-such conditions of temperature and atmosphere obtain. It is within his power to do it. Do I attribute to him, the person, the power to do something, in some sense of 'power to do,' which is not applicable to a part of his body, for example his leg, of which I might say that it can this morning withstand such-and-such pressures without breaking? My suggestion is that in the case of the physical, mindless object, his leg, there is no difference between 'will this morning withstand the pressures that will be applied' and 'can this morning withstand the pressures that will be applied,' *unless* I am using 'can' as a substitute for 'may' or 'might.' But in the case of the man, and of the action of climbing the mountain, there is a difference, and I need not be using 'can' as an alternative to 'may' or 'might'. The fact that the man failed in his attempt to climb the mountain is not by itself sufficient to establish that he could not do so. One needs the assumption that he still wanted to, and, consequently, that he was trying to, and that his failure was not attributable to lack of will. Granted this assumption, and only granted this, and given that the normal background conditions presupposed are not suddenly changed, it does indeed follow from the fact that the performance was in fact a failure that the power was at that moment lacking.

I have chosen a strained and provocative example, in which the assumption of the necessary will would ordinarily seem unavoidable, and scarcely an assumption at all; it seems improbable that he would want to lie down amid the snow and ice, and this is why the two questions 'Can he?' and 'Will he?' in this selected case seem to lie so close together. Observing the man's performance would normally, in such a case of a test or feat, be sufficient to establish whether the power exists or not, just because, in the setting of a feat, and of a test of an ability, the implied condition of a will to achieve is generally satisfied.

There are circumstances in which it would be normal to say to a man 'You can climb it if you try', or 'You could climb it if you wanted to;' he might just give up, and not try, and he might succeed in climbing just *because* he had made the wilful effort. There is no analogous assumption of a will or want required in establishing the pressure-sustaining properties of his leg, as they exist this morning. In the case of the leg, the difference between 'It cannot' and 'It will not' is that he who says that it cannot withstand the pressures alleges that it is impossible that it should withstand the pressures, or that it is certain that it will not. He makes a stronger statement, which needs to be supported by stronger grounds, than the mere prediction that it will not withstand the pressures. The grounds for such a claim to certainty will ordinarily be found in some well-confirmed causal explanation of the operations of his leg.

That there should be this difference between the man's action and the workings of his leg is not surprising; for the normal scheme of explanation of a human action—the normal answer to the question 'Why did he do it?—is in terms of his wants and interests. When a causal question is raised about his actions, it is more commonly a question of why he can, or cannot, do something, of the necessary conditions of his having the power to do it. We look for a scientific understanding of men's powers, and of their successes and failures in doing what they want to do. On what conditions do their powers to do so-and-so depend, why do they come and go, and why are they distributed among men as they are? This is the point at which a causal, and fully scientific explanation, of behaviour has a clear purpose and utility. We do hope to be able to calculate the antecedent conditions necessary for a man's success in certain performances, should he want to do

21

such-and-such, and the conditions in which he will fail; we expect this to be a domain of natural law, in which reliable uniformities will be discovered by experiment. As the result of a vast accumulation of commonplace experience, we already know, or have well-founded beliefs, about what we can, and cannot, do under under various relevant conditions. But we expect this knowledge to be extended, and our beliefs to be corrected, by more exact and controlled experiment and by the elaboration of psychological theory.

When, following the question, 'Why can X do so-and-so, while Y cannot?,' we ask 'Why does X want to do so-and-so, while Y does not?,' this second demand for explanation normally receives a different kind of answer. We will normally turn to the reasons that he has for wanting to do so-and-so, that is, to the place of this particular interest in the whole system of his desires and interests; and we can know very little of his less rudimentary wants unless we know something of his thoughts. He wants to do so-and-so, because he thinks that it is a case of so-and-so, and perhaps also because he calculates that it will lead to so-and-so. If the thoughts and beliefs are changed, the desires will normally change also. We therefore normally hope to change and to extend a man's desires and interests, and intend that our own will be changed and extended, principally by reasoning and by the force of argument; and we may admit that, failing these, they are sometimes changed by rhetoric and persuasion. For this reason, an experimental answer to the question 'Why do people of such-and-such a kind or under such-and-such conditions want to do so-and-so?,' taken as a demand for the cause, or sufficient conditions, of their desire, seems strange; for it seems that any adequate answer would specify the cause of their having certain thoughts and beliefs, and this in turn seems strange. If a man wants to do something for some reason that he has, then there is a thought on which his desire is dependent, in the sense that, if he were convinced that the belief was mistaken,

22

he would at least reconsider whether he wanted to act as he had wanted to. One can intelligibly look for causal explanations of a man's mistakes in reasoning, that is, one can look outside the reasoning process itself for a factor that explains its assuming the form that it did. But the steps in a clear and correct process of reasoning need no further explanation outside the process itself. A further explanation could only be of his ability to reason correctly, on this particular occasion. If the argument that he accepts is evidently valid, if the action that he wants to perform is evidently delightful, if the object that he fears is evidently dangerous, we do not ask for a further explanation, for a cause of his accepting the argument, wanting to act, or fearing. For this would be to question a truism. The more natural application of the scientific and causal type of explanation is, first, to the unwilled features of behaviour, and secondly, to men's powers to act in certain ways when they want to.

To summarise: The existence or non-existence of the power to do a specific thing at a particular moment can be conclusively established by actual performance in the normal conditions presupposed, but, subject to the condition that an attempt that fails establishes lack of power, only if the subject really at that time wanted to perform the action in question and was not diverted by some stronger interest. One needs to know the aims of a person in order to be sure that his not doing something is a case of his being unable to do it. The ultimate test of my ability to do something at a particular moment is 'experiment,' in the sense of my seriously trying, with a will to succeed.

I am not arguing that there is anything easy and unproblematic about the distinction between lack of the will to do something and lack of the power to do it, as this distinction is applied in particular cases, and especially in the context of moral argument, of censure, regret, and the assessment of responsibility. On the contrary, it is notoriously difficult, even if one is untroubled by theoretical doubts, to apply in particular cases the ordinary distinction between failures to do something, which are cases of lack of will to do it, and failures that justify saying, 'I cannot do it,' or 'He cannot do it.' It is easy enough to say that failure, when we make the attempt with a strong desire to succeed, shows that we could not at that moment do it. If I certainly wanted to do the thing in question very much, and if I made the attempt and failed, this would in all normal circumstances establish beyond reasonable doubt the truth of the categorical statement that I could not do it, that I was unable to do it, at that moment. Perhaps I have in general the capacity to do it, and perhaps I could *have* done it on that occasion, if such-and-such conditions, within me or in the environment, had been different. But the fact remains that I could not do it, that I was unable to do it, at that moment, where the phrase 'at that moment' is shorthand for 'all the conditions being what they were at that moment.' If lack of will is excluded, lack of power is the only account that can be given of my not doing it, given that I made the attempt. But I may on occasion be deceived about the strength and direction of my own desires and interests, and even more obviously, and often, be deceived about the desires and interests of others. And these errors about dispositions must lead to complementary errors about powers. My not doing it, or my failing to do it, may look like a case of inability, and yet, more closely scrutinised, it may turn out to be a case of not fully wanting to do it, and therefore of not really trying to do it. 'It is not true that he was unable to do it; he did not really want to and the attempt was half-hearted. He could have done it, if he had really wanted to, and wanted enough.' But we would start to talk, and to think, idly, if we made the notion of a power entirely untestable and indeterminate, by pressing the notion of wanting beyond its normal conditions of application.

Suggested re-drawings of this line between 'He would not'

and 'He could not' have always entered into controversy about conduct. When I would normally say that I did not want to do something, which I could have done, if I had wanted to, how do I know that I have not been deceived by ignorance of the specific conditions on which the ability depends? This is a questioning of the adequacy of the commonplace inductive tests of powers by parallel cases. Presented with a contrary-to-fact conditional statement of the kind 'I could have done it at that moment if I had wanted to,' it is often not unreasonable to doubt whether the apparently parallel cases really are relevantly parallel. More exact, systematic, and controlled experiment might reveal an unsuspected condition on which the ability depends. Alternatively, the revision can be made in the opposite direction, as, for example, by Sartre, with the suggestion that many cases of failing to do something, because of an alleged inability, are to be counted as cases of lack of will to do it. When, exhausted on the mountain, I say 'I cannot take another step,' Sartre suggests that I ought rather to say something like 'I prefer to sit down rather than painfully continue to walk.' These proposals for a thorough-going conceptual revision properly have a systematic and metaphysical basis, which I am omitting. But they do make contact at certain points with the apparent incoherencies and complacencies of ordinary usage and belief. Psychologists may persuade us, in the light of new experimental evidence, to question the normal methods of distinction, and may reclassify many apparent cases of lack of ability as 'really' cases of lack of desire. Simultaneously, they revise the criteria attached to 'He wanted,' or of 'He really wanted to do so-and-so,' with the suggestion that there are repressed and normally unconscious desires, which are to be discovered and identified only in certain special circumstances.

This is one point at which there seems to be geniune difficulty in sustaining the distinction. For can it not be suggested that I am sometimes unable to do something, particularly when the

inability is a symptom of neurosis, because of some unconscious desire, where the 'because' marks a causal connection?
I made the attempt and I found that I could not do it; but
perhaps only because of some conflicting desire, which I didn't
know that I had. And does not this causal dependence of the
inability on the desire prevent us from classifying the failure
as definitely either a case of inability, or as a case of lack of
will, if these two are mutually exclusive alternatives? Certainly this kind of case does prevent us from regarding the
alternative accounts of failure as in all cases mutually
exclusive. There are inabilities at particular moments, which
are identified as such by failure in an attempt, that has been
made with a conscious will to do the action in question. But
often a man's desires may be confused, ambiguous and conflicting, and the confusions of desire may be at the time
unrecognised, and unrecognisable, by the agent; then an inability may sometimes co-exist with, and be explained by, an
unconscious, or repressed, wish not to do what the agent can
also be truly said to have tried to do with a conscious will to
succeed. He showed and felt a desire to succeed, which is
sufficient to justify the statement that he could not at that
moment do what he tried to do; but perhaps it is also true that
not all his desires pointed in the same direction; and this fact
may explain his powerlessness at that moment. We do often
speak of the existence of a will to do, or to achieve, something
as a condition of the existence of the ability to do it. And men
may commonly hope to extend the apparent limits of their own
powers by further appeals to will, or by incitement of the will
of others. Once again, it is speech, and the possibilities of
incitement, exhortation and appeals to the will, which give
a place to a partially indeterminate notion of the will in the
explanation of conduct. A man may both explore the limits,
and extend the limits, of his powers by questioning his
apparent will to succeed.

I am certainly not suggesting that the line of distinction

between *vouloir* and *pouvoir,* between lack of will and lack of power, is clear and immutable in its application to human actions. I am suggesting that 'can do' and 'cannot do' is a different kind of 'can' from that of 'can happen' and 'cannot happen,' when the former is applied to creatures who may know, form, reflect on, and criticise their own occasional desires and aims, and who may, or may not, disclose them to others. The fact that men may authoritatively disclose their desires and aims, and more fundamentally, that they are capable of reflection, and that they may find *reasons* for wanting to do one thing rather than another, entails the consequence that the existence and nature of these desires and aims are not established solely, or even primarily, by observation of their actual behaviour. We need to know how they think of the actions which they want to perform. Animals complicate the issue, because we do properly attribute desires to them. But their desires and aims, linked with the necessary concomitants of desire, namely, pleasure and pain, are unformulated and are not mediated by thought; so we are prepared, in our unsentimental moments, to establish the nature of their desires solely by reference to their observable behaviour; and perhaps we are even ready to take statements about their wants as *equivalent* to some set of hypothetical statements about their observable behaviour. But we cannot accurately specify the more sophisticated desires of men without knowledge of their thoughts.

Machines have powers attributed to them, and we now often compare their powers with human powers very directly. About a particular machine, at a particular time, we may say that it can now play chess better than a particular man can. My suggestion is that the 'cans' on either side of this comparison are different in important respects. Of the particular machine, it cannot in principle be true that it can now, and at this moment, play better than the man, if, when it is now tested in action under the normal conditions presupposed, it in fact plays worse. Of the machine we may, of course, say that it *could* play better than the man, or that it *could have* played better, that it has unrealised potentialities, potentialities which would be realised under different conditions, either inside the machine itself, or outside it. But this is not to make the plain categorical statement that this particular machine can now play better, conditions inside and outside the machine being what they now in fact are. If it can now play better, it will play better, when it is tested under the normally presupposed conditions. Contrast the man: it is in principle possible that he can now play better than the machine, even though, when he is observed in action, he in fact plays worse. He may not want to play better, and therefore he may not try to; perhaps he prefers at this time to leave his ability unused, and prefers not to play as well as he can. This cannot be true of the machine; its powers, or potentialities, are merely that which it *would* observably do under certain implied or stated conditions.

Suppose a machine that is programmed to make a losing move whenever its human opponent makes a foolish, losing move. Of this machine on this occasion, playing against a bad player, we can say 'It cannot win now.' It is certain that it will lose. Sufficient conditions of its defeat already exist in its programming. Contrast a man, a good player, who very much wants to save his opponent humiliation; there is a good sense in which he can win, but it is certain that he won't. We know two categorical statements about him to be true: (1) that he has the power to win, and (2) that he is determined, firmly intends, not to use his power. I am not denying that to a machine may be attributed powers and potentialities to do various things at particular moments, powers that may come and go, as the conditions on which they depend are varied. But to establish the existence of a machine's power to do something at a particular moment, and under the conditions then obtaining, it is both necessary and sufficient to

28

provide the standard and appropriate input, or stimulus, which is required for the realisation of this power, and to wait for the appropriate response in performance. In the case of establishing the existence of a man's power to do something at a particular moment, this is not sufficient. There is one *overriding* condition that must be known to be satisfied before the equivalent test of performance is accepted as decisive: that the subject wants, or has the will, to pass the test. If this peculiar, internal condition is not known to be satisfied, failure in present performance does not prove inability.

J. L. Austin, in his published British Academy Lecture 'Ifs and Cans,' made the point that 'I can do so-and-so now,' and 'I can do so-and-so now, if I want' or 'if I choose,' are categorical statements. I shall not repeat the argument. The important point here is that 'I can do so-and-so now' is the form of words that we typically use when a feat, something involving, or thought to involve, the possibility of failure, is in question. You may predict, or bet, that I cannot escape from a certain position, and I may predict, or bet, that I can; in this setting of a challenge to a feat, where the will to succeed is assumed, 'can' is scarcely distinguishable from 'will succeed, if I make the attempt.' My statement is conclusively verified, and yours conclusively falsified, if I do escape when I make the attempt. If I do not then escape, the contradictory is true. Having failed, I still may argue that I *could have* escaped, using a form of words that implies I would have been able to escape, if some missing condition had been satisfied: I could have, if I had been more careful, or if I had not been distracted, or even if I had tried harder; for 'trying' can also be included among the conditions of success. 'You can if you try, but you will not be able to, unless you try' is a familiar causal judgment. Equally familiar—'Why cannot I do it?' (said by a golfer, or by a pianist, or by someone trying to remember a name): 'Well, you would be able to do it if you didn't try so hard: just don't try, you will find that you can do it.' 'Try,' as it occurs in these causal judgments, has a rather different use and implication from the 'try' which means 'make an attempt to'—in French, *essayer,* or H. A. Prichard's 'set oneself to.' I may make either a half-hearted or a serious attempt to do something. I may set about it with a will to succeed, or without any real desire to succeed. In the causal judgments, 'You can do it, if you try: but you will not be able to do it unless you try,' 'try' implies something like 'make an effort to'—the use of 'try' that William James stressed in his chapter on the will. But when I say, contradicting you, 'I can raise this glass without spilling the wine,' and when in this context I intend this to be scarcely distinguishable from 'I will succeed if I try,' the 'try' does not imply 'make an effort.' If I make the attempt and fail, I have to admit that you were right when you said 'You cannot do it now.' Perhaps I *could have,* if I had not been over-confident, and if I had not thought that I could do it without taking trouble; but the fact remains that I *could not* at that moment, as things were, with my over-confidence included in the conditions at that moment. Perhaps you knew me well enough to gamble on my over-confidence, and that is why you said 'You cannot do it.' When I ask you whether you can now remember the first lines of *Paradise Lost,* and you answer that you can, you claim that you will succeed on this particular occasion. In the peculiar setting of a challenge to a feat, or to a test of ability, 'can' and 'will succeed' almost coincide, because the will to succeed is assumed. In other settings of inquiry into your powers, I am normally asking what you would succeed in doing if you really wanted to and really tried, that is, made the attempt with an unqualified desire to succeed.

It is important to notice that, if we learn what we can do by trying, the slipperiness, amounting almost to ambiguity, in the notion of 'trying' must infect the notion of a man's power to do something with an equivalent slipperiness. We do normally, in reviewing actions, include the existence of an unqualified desire to do something in the conditions that must be satisfied before the power to do something on a particular occasion has been proved not to exist. In some contexts and for some purposes—for example, those of the stern moralist—we may say that a man can only be known to be unable to do something, if it has been proved that he fails, when all the internal conditions are favourable; that is, when he has strongest possible desire to do the thing in question, and when there are no conflicting desires of any kind. In other contexts and for other purposes—e.g. of challenges and bets—we may take the weaker test as decisive —'conditions being what they are, in your mind and elsewhere, you will not succeed, if you make the attempt now.' There is not any firm and general rule that prescribes the background of standing conditions presupposed in the test of powers and potentialities, either of persons or of things. The background of conditions presupposed will vary with the situation in which a man's powers are being judged, and with the purposes for which the judgment is needed. I shall be mainly concerned in this book with the situation of a man who, before acting, has to decide what to do, and, secondarily, with that of a man who advises him about his decision, taking into account, as they both must, the limits of the agent's powers, as they exist on a particular occasion. In this situation, in which an estimate needs to be made as a guide to future action, 'You (or I) can do so-and-so' is conclusively verified or falsified when an attempt is made with a full conscious desire to succeed, and without any conscious conflict of desire: even though a subsequent acceptable explanation of the failure might refer to an unconscious desire to fail.

It is sometimes implied that we must wait upon science, and the discovery of causal laws, to know what men can and cannot do, as we must wait upon science and the discovery of causal laws to learn about the powers of metals and gases. But this is not true. I unavoidably acquire an immense amount of knowledge about what I can and cannot do, directly, and in the ordinary course of existence, in my attempts, achievements, and failures. Certainly scientific investigation of the necessary conditions upon which these powers depend will greatly add to this knowledge, and will permit reliable inferences, far beyond the range of direct experience, to an estimate of what my powers would be under various specified conditions. And much more important, such investigation will enable me to find the means of increasing my powers to act in specific ways in specific kinds of situation. No conceivable advances in scientific knowledge can lead to the conclusion that I am not often—for example, at this moment—confronted with a plurality of things that I can do if I want to, between which I must choose: that there is this plurality of open possibilities I know by experience, as surely as I know anything, including the laws of physics and psychology.

To summarise:

We make a mistake if we interpret 'He cannot act differently' as parallel to 'This gas cannot behave differently.' 'There is no possibility of his acting differently' is indeed parallel to 'This gas cannot behave differently,' where this latter is interpreted to mean, 'It is certain that this gas will not behave differently.' 'He cannot act differently' neither entails, nor is entailed by, 'There is no possibility of his acting differently.' The entailment that does hold is between 'There is no possibility that he will be able to act differently' (i.e. 'It is certain that he will not be able to') and 'There is no possibility that he will act differently.' It may be certain that a man will not do X because it is certain that he will not want to do X; but it does not follow that there are no possibilities other than X which are open to him, in the sense that there is nothing that he can do. The notion of a power, as applied to men, depends on the twin notion of 'want,' or 'will,' used in the explanation of action, when the will, or desire, to do something on a particular occasion may be formed, discovered, reflected upon, criticised, and formulated, and perhaps also disclosed to others.

## Chapter 2

## DESIRE

The argument has proceeded as follows: (1) powers to act in specific ways at specific moments are attributable to creatures who may, or may not, want to act in those specific ways at those specific moments, and who may identify, and declare, their wants. (2) Such powers to act may be known to exist at specific moments, and may be identified, independently of the methods by which we identify the corresponding powers of things, e.g. machines, and of animals. When we definitely, and without qualification or conflict, want to do something at a particular moment, sincerely make the attempt in normal conditions, and yet fail, we know, as surely as we can ever know, that at that moment we could not do it. He who failed in the attempt under these conditions was not in a position to do it, literally or metaphorically, or he lacked the means, or the ability, at that particular moment. This conclusive falsification of 'He can,' or 'He could,' gives the peculiar force of 'He can', when applied to creatures who have desires, and who may know what they are, and who may report them, reflect on them and criticise them. But this account is incomplete, unless some account is also given of wanting, and of being inclined, or of having an impulse, at a specific time to do a specific thing. This is the type of case of wanting to do something with which we are concerned: not with unspecific, long range and so-called dispositional uses of the term: but with specific desires and inclinations to act in a determinate way on a particular occasion. At a particular moment I may want to laugh, or I may be inclined to weep. I may have an impulse to run away, or need to restrain myself from striking the man in front of me. These are primary dispositions to act that I feel, and that occur as episodes in my biography, no less than my sensations and actions. Even though they remain, unexpressed, as episodes in my inner life, not perceptible by observers, they are accounted episodes, occurrences, not possible happenings only.

It makes sense to speak of animals, who do not themselves identify and declare their wants, as wanting to do things on particular occasions. But their desire to do a particular thing on a particular occasion is revealed in, or inferred from, their behaviour. If the desire is directly revealed in behaviour, it is revealed in their attempting, and either succeeding or failing, to do something. To speak here of their attempting to do something is ordinarily to speak of the purpose that explains a segment of their behaviour by reference to a goal. With animals we recognise their desire to do certain things in their attempts to do them, and in the signs of dissatisfaction when they are stopped. Desire, even at the most primitive level, is linked not only to behaviour, in an ordinary and non-technical sense of that word, but also to pleasure and pain; 'linked,' in the sense that it is a constitutive condition of desiring to do something that the subject, other things being equal, is in some degree pleased when the opportunity of doing it is presented to him, and to some degree pained or displeased, other things being equal, when the opportunity is taken away. The connection between the concepts is a two-way connection: as the existence of a desire to do something may be established, at least in part, by noticing that the creature is pleased or displeased, other things being equal, by the arrival or removal of opportunities of doing it: so also the fact that a creature derives pleasure or pain from doing certain things may be established, at least in part and to some degree, by noticing that it wants to do, or to avoid doing, those things.

The third feature of desire, and particularly of the desire to act, that needs to be noticed is that desires are in their nature liable to conflict. It is intrinsic to the notion of desire, at all levels, that a creature may at any time simultaneously desire to do things that cannot simultaneously be done, and to do things that are felt as conflicting and contradictory by the creature itself, as may be evidenced by its starting-and-stopping behaviour. Hence the phrase 'other things being equal,' which always creeps into discussions of desire. In this sense desires are, as such, conditional. But a statement to the effect that someone desires to do such-and-such is not a conditional statement, or reducible to, or equivalent to, a determinate conditional statement. 'A wants to do X' is indeed equivalent to 'other things being equal, he would do X, if he could.' But the open, or catch-all, phrase 'other things being equal' in the protasis cannot be replaced by a definite condition, or closed set of conditions, without destroying the equivalence. It is of the nature of desire that a desire or interest may at any time be prevented from issuing in action by a conflicting desire or interest. The desire to act in a specific way may remain latent and unexpressed, even when there is an opportunity of gratifying it; and there is no finite list of alternative explanations of a person's behaviour which must be true, as of logical necessity, under these conditions of conflict. The explanation of human conduct in terms of desires and interests leaves a margin of indeterminacy. For this reason those who hope to explain human conduct by methods that are appropriate to explaining the operations of a machine already know that they will dispense with the concept of desire. But they will have difficulty in dispensing with, or accounting for, the first person uses of the verb—'I want so-and-so, and therefore I will do so-and-so'—when a man first decides what he wants, and then, in the light of this, decides what he will do.

There must be some detectable relation between a man's desires and his performances; but in a human being, as contrasted with an animal, it is not a precise and simple relation; for wants and wishes may come and go, and linger, out of sight, in a human mind, and be felt, concealed and declared, and be disconnected from coarse achievement, as dreams may be, or hopes, or mere pleasurable picturings; they still may help to explain the odd things that one visibly does. Because a desire may be the object of reflection, for men though not for animals, it may be disconnected from its natural and immediate expression in behaviour, either when there are conflicting desires, or when there is no opportunity of acting in accordance with the desire.

From Aristotle onwards it has been clear that the existence of a desire to do something is independent of the capacity to identify the desire as a desire of a certain kind, and independent also of the capacity to form a desire as the outcome of a communicable process of thought. Wanting—unlike, for example, regretting—is not an essentially thought-dependent, and therefore an essentially human, concept. It is not restricted in its application to language-users, who can think of the object of their desire as being of a certain kind. Sexual desire, lust in any of its common forms, the desire of the hungry man for food, or of the thirsty man for drink, and some desires that arise from other bodily needs, may come into existence independently of any conception: either on sight of a particular thing that I immediately want, and feel inclined to pursue, or as the effect of causes unknown to me; I may merely look and want, and not know why, as I may look and pursue, and not know why. Desire presupposes only the capacity to act and to feel; and an animal's wants, and an infant's desires, are no less wants, and in no weaker sense wants, than the fully articulated desires which emerge from reflection. But the capacity to think about, and to characterise our wants, necessarily introduces new complexities into the identification of them. In this respect wants and purposes are alike: neither are essentially thought-dependent concepts, as are the concepts of doubt, regret, and intention. Both wants and purposes can be ascribed to creatures who have not the capacity to reflect upon them and to report them.

The capacity to reflect upon what one wants to do, and to make up one's mind about what one wants to do, and to come to know what one wants to do, carries with it the capacity to communicate one's desire to do something; and the capacity to communicate a desire to do something carries with it the power to review the desire, to ask questions about it, and to criticise it as misguided. Self-consciousness, the awareness of the possibility of mistake, and the power to communicate go together, all three; it is a mistake to think of one or the other as primary in explaining the methods of confirmation appropriate to, and therefore the sense, of psychological concepts. One's desire to act in certain ways becomes something that one may reflect upon, criticise, and abandon, *because of* the criticism, and not merely something that one has, as one has a sensation. Desires do not only occur; they may also be formed, and formed as the outcome of a process of criticism. Therefore one has reasons for wanting to act in certain ways. Because the notions of correctness and incorrectness, of right and wrong, are in place, the notions of 'a reason for,' and of 'my reason for' and 'his reason for,' are also in place. And whenever the notion of my, or his, reason for is in place, some notion of mistake is also in place. There are my reasons for believing so-and-so; my reasons for doing such-and-such: for wanting to do so-and-so: for liking such-and-such: for regretting: for being angry with, or frightened of, such-and-such, and so on. These are all things in which I may be misguided, and in respect of which I may deviate from some norm or standard of appropriateness. A sensation cannot be correct or incorrect, right or wrong. There is only the fact that it occurs or that it does not occur. The question 'Why?,' asked in respect of a sensation, cannot be interpreted as an invitation to justify having the sensation, to show that it is not inappropriate and to give a reason, as opposed to discovering a cause; one cannot be asked to rebut a charge of misguidedness. But if a man can identify his desires to act in certain ways as satisfying certain descriptions, and can therefor reflect upon them, he may also evaluate and criticise them. They are his, in a strong sense of authorship, and he may take responsibility for them. His character, as Aristotle remarks, is as much a matter of his desires as of his overt doings. He may find reasons for them, and be ready to defend them as having appropriate objects. If he is persuaded that the actions that he wanted to perform are misguided, and that they would be unpleasant and inexpedient, he must have *some* desire not to do that which he first wanted, or that he has wanted, to do. He is in a position to deliberate about the possible objects of his desire, and to think whether he is right to want to do X rather than Y; and this thinking may be distinguishable from thinking about what he will do, since the setting may be one in which no one of the possibilities under consideration is taken to be a practical possibility at the time. I can distinguish thinking about what I want to do from practical thinking about what I will do, when I know or believe that, for one reason or another, there is no present possibility of my actually doing any of the things considered, or when I disregard the practical possibilities. If on a particular occasion I consider only the hypothetical question of what I would do, if I could, the conclusion at which I arrive would normally represent my prevailing will or desire in the matter (*voluntas, volonté*); or, if the will or desire is shown to be wholly impracticable, my mere wish. The normal case of deciding, after deliberation, what I want to do is a case of making a practical decision, but one which is conditional in form. To decide that I want to do X is normally to decide that I will do X, if there is the opportunity and the means to do X, and if there is no overriding reason of a quite different kind, independent of my present desires and interests, for not doing X.

Any reasons that I have for wanting to do X are also reasons for me to do X: but I might have reasons for doing

X which are not reasons for my wanting to do X. It is not a truism that, if I did X, I had some reason for wanting to do it. In spite of Aristotle, it is not obviously impossible that a man might have reasons for doing X that have nothing to do with his own desires or interests. The agent might, for example, think that he *must* do X, or that he ought to do X, in spite of the fact that he does not want, in any normal sense of the word, to do anything of the kind. Perhaps he has to 'make' himself do X, in spite of the fact that he does not in the least want to do it. Nor is it a truism that there must be something which he wants, and which is such that he believes that doing X is a necessary condition of obtaining it, or is at least a means of obtaining it. But it does seem a necessary truth that if for some reason I want to do X, I have some reason for doing X, whether I actually do X or not. Of course it is not a necessary truth that, if I want to do X, there is a reason why I want to do it: I might just want to do something e.g. to sleep or to eat, and yet there be no reason why I want to do this. I just want to do something, the impulse in such a case occurs without reflection, as a sensation occurs; the desire terminates in its object, which, in the cases we are considering, is an action or activity. But the impulse that occurs in such cases may always be made the object of reflection and criticism. There may have been originally no reason for my wanting to do the thing in question, and the only explanation of the original occurrence of the impulse may be found in some conditions external to my mind. I may, on reflection, want, and have reasons for wanting, to be free from this desire.

These are the features of the concept of the desire to act which have been noticed, and variously emphasised, since Aristotle. First, there is the link between desire and pleasure, and between pain and the desire to avoid; all and only creatures that have these elementary feelings can be said to have desires, and all creatures that have desires can be said to have these feelings. Secondly, there is the link between desire and having a reason for doing something. Thirdly, many writers have remarked that it is essential to desires and interests that there should be conflicts of desire and interest in the minds of persons, which may be inferred from their behaviour. There is a fourth feature of the concept of desire, applied to creatures who have the power to reflect, which, again with varying emphasis, has generally been recognised in the literature: the link between something being desired, in a certain way or under certain conditions, by human beings, and that thing or activity being in some way good, or its being thought to be good. From Aristotle until the present day various accounts of this connection have been suggested. Whatever may be in detail the correct account of it, there is some necessary connection between being reflectively desired and being thought to be good, and between being desired and being valued, more or less highly. At least Aristotle was right, as against some modern writers, to imply that, he who says 'X is a good novel' or 'X is a good administrator,' using the word 'good' attributively, is committed to the following proposition—'If it is really a novel (or administrator) that you want, X is one of the things that you particularly want,' with the implication that, if the speaker rejects this book or person as not being what he wants, he has not specified the exact nature of his desire correctly and completely; it is not, strictly speaking, a desire for a novel or an administrator, but for some differently, or more fully, characterised type of book or person. He who says 'Security is a good thing,' and 'It is a good thing that men should have leisure,' using the word 'good' predicatively, is committed to the proposition that it is desirable that security and leisure should, among other things, exist, and that he who does not want them to exist is misguided in his desires. These then are the accepted, rudimentary features of the concept of wanting, in the setting of action and of the explanation of actions.

On these foundations the complexities of a human being identifying what he wants to do on a particular occasion, and of communicating his desires, are superimposed. For there are great complexities; a reflective creature's knowing what he wants, and his not knowing what he wants, may take many different forms. I may misrepresent the objects of my interest, both in my own mind and in talking to others, and my wants may also be inchoate and confused in themselves. Knowing what one wants, like knowing what one is doing, or knowing what one is going to do, has its own peculiarities as a form of knowledge. First, there is the institution of asking to do something in the first person singular, either in the present or the future tense, of the verb 'want'; in the appropriate circumstances this type of utterance would not be intended to evoke belief, or to be judged as either true or false. In the appropriate circumstances such an utterance would constitute either a request, or an act of choice, or a formal notice of future action, or something like this; it would not constitute a statement that might be mistaken in just those ways that statements are mistaken, by being evidently in conflict with the facts, or by being ill-founded or unjustified.

This feature of the concept of want—that the first person singular of the present or future tense of the verb has a non-statement-making function in some circumstances—is common to many, and perhaps to most, psychological concepts. The exact nature of this function is always to be interpreted as a further feature of the psychological concept, alongside the conditions of its application in statements supposed to be true. This first person use is not to be thought of as a quite disconnected or deviant use of the verb. That utterances of the form 'I want to do so-and-so' are commonly requests for permission to act, or for opportunity to act, or for something very like this, throws light on the sense of the statement 'I want to do so-and-so,' when these words are intended to convey information, which must be either true or false information. He who wants to do something is so far ready, other things being equal, to undertake to do it. And so it very naturally comes about that just saying 'I want' is taken as a way of seeking an opportunity, just as saying 'I intend' is taken as a way of giving an undertaking. As a point of philosophical principle, it seems wrong to give priority either to the first-person performative, or semi-performative, uses of the phrase, or to the statement-making uses. Both uses are characteristic and they are mutually dependent. In a discussion of freedom of mind, one is more concerned with the statement-making uses of the phrase, with the application of the concept by a person in true or false avowals of his own wants, and in his attributing wants to others. One is concerned with the setting in which 'I want to do X,' and 'It is not the case that I want to do X,' are statements parallel, and analogous, to 'I can do X' and 'I cannot do X' (which may also, but more rarely, be given a quasi-performative use). Of the man who wants to do X at time T, tries to do it, and fails to do it, or fails in doing it, it must normally be true that he could not do it at T. This normally conclusive test of the presence or absence of an ability to do something at a particular time is applicable only to creatures who have feelings of pleasure and pain, and not to machines. We do not yet have a clear, and perhaps not even a vague, conception of what would count as discovering, or fabricating, something which we would have good reasons for calling a machine, and to which we would also have good reasons for attributing feelings of pleasure and of pain. To assert this is not to assert either (a) that we can demonstrate that the notion of a machine that has feelings contains an explicit contradiction, or (b) that we can know in advance that there will never be grounds for revising our classificatory scheme, and for recognising a category of things which are in their nature intermediate between machines, as we know them, and creatures that have feelings of pleasure and pain.

43

Among creatures who have wants there is a conspicuous difference between those creatures whose wants are revealed only in their behaviour, and in signs of pleasure and pain, and those whose wants, directed toward an action or activity, may also be quite otherwise identified: identified directly by the subjects themselves, who reflect upon, and decide, what they want to do. Those, and only those, who may reflect on their wants, and who may also report them, can have desires to act at determinate dates remote from the immediate present. Only through the use of concepts do I have a world of interests that is extended in time. And only language-users can follow a norm requiring consistency in their wants over a period of time, and can correct their wants by reference to a standard of consistency in their interests.

The transition from 'I do not know what I want to do now' to 'I now do know what I want to do' is one transition, involving one set of liabilities to error, and the transition from 'I do not know what he wants to do now' to 'I now do know what he wants to do' is another transition, involving some of the same liabilities to error, but involving also different ones. In respect of knowledge of one's desires, the subject is the normal authoritative source, although he is liable to error and although he may be corrected by an observer. In respect of desires, as also of sensations, the subject is the authoritative source of knowledge, in the sense that the question 'How does X know?' is out of place in respect of any statement about desires or feelings, when X is both the author of the statement and the designated subject of the statement. Only an observer can intelligibly be asked to give the *source* of his knowledge of a man's desires and feelings. The subject can be asked 'Are you sure?,' and he may be reproached with errors of various kinds, against which he may have failed to take precautions. 'Are you sure?' asks him whether he has taken all possible precautions against misinterpretation and misrepresentation of his desires. I may not acknowledge my own desires; I may be grossly or subtly self-deceived about them: I may not like to think, or to recognise, that I want to do so-and-so. I may sometimes discover, to my surprise, that I have for a long time wanted to do something without my having been aware that I wanted to do this. I may characterise my desires wrongly in various different ways, either in silent reflection or in communicating them to others. Lastly, I may know (in one sense) what I want to do more or less clearly, and yet may give, in communicating with others, the wrong description of what I want to do, using the wrong names.

There is a fundamental difficulty in the direct identification of many of our desires. We may on occasion painfully discover and identify desires to act in a specific way on a specific occasion that we had previously excluded, as we now recognise, from our consciousness; and we may even discover that the desires, which we had professed, were the exact opposite of the desires, which, after painful investigation, we would now say that we actually had, although we did not know it at the time. There are various techniques of introspection, in conjunction with more careful observation of our behaviour, from which we may learn that there is often a confusion of wishes and inclinations within us, and that apparent desires may mask a real desire to act in a quite different way. We discover that our desires are often confused, and that it is often difficult to find the truth when we make statements about what we want to do; and lastly, we discover that the truth about the objects of desire is often complex, and that we have motives for concealing this complexity from ourselves and from others.

Inquiring into the desires of others, I may know (in one sense) what someone wants to do, and yet use the wrong description in stating what he wants to do. And this may be a trivial, or an untrivial, mistake of calling some person, thing, or activity, by the wrong name. Perhaps the wrong name shows a substantial misconception of what he has in mind, or perhaps it is mere ignorance of the correct name or description: or the error may be intermediate between these two. A desire is often mediated by a description of the action or activity desired. If it is mediated by a description, then any entirely correct account of what the subject wants to do must include that same description, or some description that is equivalent to it, or that is implied by it. If the desire is not mediated by a description, there is no such restriction in identifying what he wants to do. The mediating description represents the subject's conception of the object, or activity, desired; and we can distinguish between cases in which the conception of the activity is essential to the existence of the desire from cases in which it is accidental.

But what does it mean to say that a desire to do something is, or is not, mediated by a description? Consider an example: 'Smith wants to buy the most expensive picture in the gallery.' Suppose that I read, or hear, this statement, and want to know whether it is true. It would be incorrect to say that the statement, the truth of which I am inquiring into, is ambiguous; perhaps it would not even be correct to say that it is, as quoted, indeterminate in sense. But there are two or more distinct states of affairs, or situations, which it might represent. It might be the case that Smith had conceived the desire of buying whatever picture happened to be the most expensive picture in the gallery. Or he might have seen a picture, which he immediately liked and wanted, and which happened to be the most expensive. In the second case, his desire to buy the picture is unmediated by this, or by any other, description of the picture: in the first case the desire to buy the picture is mediated by the description, which is essential to the desire, and specifies the exact nature of the desire. The two desires are entirely different and reveal very different characters; but the same form of words may truthfully represent both these situations. And of course this form of words might represent various other situations intermediate between these two.

In this simplified example the contrast is clear. But there can be a great variety of less simple cases in which a desire to do something is mediated by the thought of the action as an action of a certain kind. A mediating description may be highly specific, and may exactly determine the nature of the action or activity desired; or the conception, on which the existence of the desire depends, may be a relatively vague conception of the activity desired. In either case, that particular desire to act would disappear, if the conception were shown to be in some way faulty or confused or unreal. Whatever the character of the conception, general or specific, vague or precise, having the desire may depend on having the conception as its necessary condition. An observer who had not grasped the conception involved would misidentify the desire. This thought-impregnated type of desire is to be contrasted with cases, at the opposite end of the scale, in which the desire to act in a particular way is independent of any thought at all. When I am starving, my desire to eat does not depend for its existence on any particular conception that I have of this activity: it depends solely on my stomach. In this second type of situation one may pass from the desire to some characterisation of it; in the contrasting type of case, the characterisation of the object leads to the desire. It is of the first importance for this inquiry that the conception of an act or activity—and in some cases even the precise words in which the conception presents itself—can be the determining factor in the formation of a desire to act. This Don Quixotism is peculiarly human, and has no place in the behaviour of animals.

The difference between the two kinds of desire is usually reflected in the manner in which the desires have been formed. When the desire to do something is essentially mediated by the description of the action or activity, the description normally contains, or implies, the ground or reason of the subject's wanting to do the thing in question. The description of the thing wanted shows what the subject wants it *for;* it singles out the feature of the thing which is of interest to him. Of the man who wanted to buy the most expensive picture in the gallery, for whom this is the essential description of what he wants to do, it is normally true that he has some reason for wanting to buy an expensive thing, e.g. that it adds to prestige, or that it is likely to be a better investment. These are reasons, in the sense that if he were persuaded that the picture brought no prestige, or that it was a bad investment, he would no longer be so sure that he wanted it. This is the sense in which the thought determines the desire, and is a condition of its existence. It would be odd, and almost unintelligible—though not any kind of misuse of the language—that he should say with apparent sincerity: 'I simply want to buy the most expensive picture: there is no particular reason why I do: I suppose I like expensive things.' The nature of the desire is so far not evident because it is abnormal, and the explanation of it is so far not evident. If the essential description were 'the most beautiful picture in the gallery,' the nature of the desire would be evident. That beauty gives pleasure is a truism. If the desire was merely to buy a particular picture which the subject had seen, and if, in specifying this desire, no description was essential, provided that it sufficiently identified the picture in the context of speech, no further explanation of the want is so far required. There may be an explanation, in the sense of a ground or reason; but there is no *need* for one. One may simply want to do something at a particular time, without the desire to do it being attributable to any line of thought or calculation. This desire to do this particular thing may not be subsumable under some other desire. Then there will be no informative answer to the question 'Why do you want to do that?,' if this is interpreted as a request for the calculation or steps which led to the formation of the desire: for there were no such steps. I would like to have the picture: or it simply gives me pleasure. That which gives pleasure is a normal object of desire.

A desire to act, essentially mediated by a description, could also be called a thought-dependent desire, as opposed to the want that terminates in the activity wanted. Where a thought is essential, disclosure by the subject has a peculiar authority, though not of course an absolute and unchallengeable authority, in identifying the desire as a desire directed towards action of a certain kind. Certainly the evidence of behaviour might be sufficient ground for belief that the statement by the agent disclosing his desire was false and mistaken; perhaps he is self-deceived, and thinks that he has given the correct account, when his behaviour in appropriate circumstances strongly indicates a different direction of interest. But the method of confirmation appropriate to statements about the typically thought-dependent desires of human beings is different from that which is appropriate to animals; and the liabilities to error are correspondingly different. With human subjects there is always the theoretical possibility, and often the real possibility, that the subject's conception of the action or activity wanted has not been correctly understood by an observer. The difficulties that are involved in reproducing correctly, and in the right terms, a man's unstated beliefs may also be involved in reproducing his conception of something that he wants to do, when the conception of the activity is essential to the desire. The observer has to infer that the subject's thoughts and calculations have followed a certain path, if the thoughts and calculations have not been faithfully presented to him in speech or writing.

Because the power to do something on a specific occasion is a function of the will to do it (for human beings), any complexities that attend the confirmation of statements involving desire also infect statements about the powers of men to act on specific occasions. Insofar as behavioural criteria are insufficient in determining what men want to do, they are insufficient also in determining what they are able to do. And since the intentional relationship is present in wanting, it enters into trying also. In knowing what someone is trying to do, one must also know how he thinks of, or conceives, his own action. The extra dimension of description is added: an observer often needs to know the agent's conception of his own action in order to know how the action is to be correctly described, at least for some purposes and in some contexts; in particular we need to know this, when our purpose is to discover whether the agent could not do what he wanted to do, and thereby to discover whether he was a free agent in this particular matter.

If an action, which one might have expected to be performed. is not performed, the usual explanation is either that the agent lacked a prevailing desire or interest, and did not really want to do it, or that he lacked the power, that he could not do it. The third possibility, which may be counted as distinct, is that he thought that he ought not to do it. This scheme of explanation is intrinsic to the commonplace concept of action. But why do we have this scheme? And is it irreplaceable?

That scheme of explanation of actions, which depends on the complementary notions of the will and of the power to act, is irreplaceable, only as long as we distinguish those desires that are thought-impregnated, and which will change when our beliefs about their objects change, and those desires which do not depend for their existence on our beliefs. If we had good reason to believe that, for *every* desire that we *ever* felt to act in some specific way on some specific occasion, there was a set of sufficient conditions to be discovered outside our own thinking, e.g. in some physical condition, we would have motives for revising our scheme of explanation of action. We might then take the occurrence of the known determining physical condition of a desire, rather than the disclosed desires themselves, with their accompanying thoughts and reasons, as the basis for predicting, and, where possible, altering, a man's actions. But the difficulty is to understand what it would mean for a man to adopt this attitude towards himself and his own desires. He who is required to decide what he wants to do, and, because he does not know or is not yet sure, must think before deciding, will consider reasons for deciding in one way rather than another. He cannot in this situation, in which he is considering the desirability of various possibilities, regard himself as waiting to *discover* or to *observe* in which direction he will be moved. In this situation of deliberation, coming to want to do X is scarcely distinguishable from coming to the conclusion that X has features which make it desirable for him to do it. The situation of a man making up his mind what he wants is a situation in which he is ready to, and is committed to, change his mind, and to cease wanting to do what he had previously wanted to do, as a result of new considerations being suggested to him; in the process of deliberation he assumes, that if his beliefs about the object were changed, his desire to act in a specific way would be changed also. As we have much better grounds for speaking of thought-dependent desires of this kind than we have for accepting any hypothesis that is incompatible with the belief that such desires exist, we so far have good reason to cling to the scheme of explanation in terms of the twin notions of the will and the power to act. We have good reason to claim that propositions of the form 'I would not want to do so-and-so, if I did not believe that so-and-so' are often true; and we have no equally good reasons to accept any scientific, or quasi-scientific, hypothesis from which it follows that no such proposition is ever true. We have the experience of being convinced by evidence and argument that our desires involve a misconception of the object or are in some way misguided, and of changing our mind as new considerations are suggested. Then the order of thoughts and of changing desires is a normal order of activity, and explains itself as normal. That a given individual had this power of active thinking at one time, and lacked it at another time, may be explained by causes external to his mind. There are explanations to be found of why his power of thought stops at a certain point, and why he makes mistakes at certain times when trying to think clearly. By acquiring this knowledge of causes, one may sometimes acquire the power to increase one's power of thought.

To conclude: he who is asked whether he wants to do X rather than Y, and who hesitates and is not sure whether he wants to do X or Y, has to think and to make up his mind; in this setting his thought will be a consideration of the reasons that make X and Y desirable things for him to do; the conclusion of his consideration will be a decision, from which a definite desire emerges. He now knows what he wants to do, because he has now formed his desire, and not because he now knows how a pre-existing desire is properly to be characterised. He is therefore authoritative when he now says 'I want to do X,' even though he is not immune from error; authoritative, not only in the sense previously noted, that he cannot intelligibly be asked 'How do you know?': also in the sense that, in virtue of having decided, he is the author of his desire. He is not in the position of a man who reports an impulse or inclination that has occurred to him, as he might report a sensation. His position, in respect of his claim to know what he wants, is more like that of a man who announces his intention.

The difference between these two kinds of claim to knowledge belongs to the next chapter.

## Chapter 3

## TWO KINDS OF KNOWLEDGE

We have two sharply distinguishable kinds of knowledge of the future. Secondly, these two kinds of knowledge are mutually dependent; it is not possible that we should possess one kind without possessing the other. There is the knowledge of the future that we possess in virtue of having formed firm intentions to act in certain ways in the immediate future, and sometimes also in the relatively remote future. I very often know, when I am speaking to you, what I am going to say next; I know how the sentence, which I am at the moment uttering, will end; and I may know this in virtue of having decided that these are the words that I shall use. Many, perhaps most, of my distinguishable actions and performances are extended in time, and I commonly know in the earlier phases of an action what the ensuing phases will be. This is the most evident type of case in which we have knowledge of the future arising from firm intentions. In the ordinary flow of a purposive action this knowledge is extended over a period of time. But I also sometimes know what I shall do on a specific occasion in the more remote future; I know in virtue of being fully determined to do it on that occasion.

The other, and, as I claim, entirely distinct kind of knowledge of the future is that which is normally to be justified by inductive reasoning and by observation of the natural course of things. Knowledge of the future of this kind is not restricted in subject matter, and may extend to my own future achievements. Knowing, as I do, the natural course of events, I know that I shall find myself doing various things that I could mention in the next days, weeks, months, and years.

The only restriction is that I cannot intelligibly justify a claim to certain knowledge of what I shall voluntarily do on a specific occasion by an inductive argument; if I do really know what I shall do, voluntarily, and entirely of my own free will, on a specific occasion, I must know this in virtue of a firm intention to act in a certain way. This is a conceptual necessity, and it helps to explain the concept of an action, which the agent performs of his own free will.

I must now try to answer those who will object that there are not two clearly distinguishable kinds of knowledge of the future: first, with a concession. He who claims to know that he will perform such-and-such a voluntary action in the future, and who claims to know this in virtue of his intention to perform it, is still liable to have his claim rebutted by inductive arguments; in this sense, and to this degree, there is an inductive component in non-inductive knowledge of the future. There are at least two typical ways in which a claim to knowledge of the future, which is not founded upon, and to be justified by, inductive reasoning, might still be rebutted by inductive considerations. The first possibility is simply that he who claims to know about his own future voluntary action on a specific occasion has not observed, or has forgotten, that something will probably, or will certainly, prevent him doing what he intends to do, and that he will, or may, lack the power, the opportunity, or the means, to do it. The statement of intention which he might have made—'I shall go by train to London tomorrow'—may be met by the statement: 'No, you will not; there are no trains tomorrow.' He did have the intention to go; but his statement purported, among other things, to be a guide to the future; and considered as a guide to the future, it was incorrect. Let us suppose that he had been asked what he intended to do tomorrow by someone who needed this information about the future course of events. The agent's answer, given in good faith, has failed to provide the information sought.

The second, more interesting, possibility is that he who claims to know what he will do tomorrow has failed to observe, or to remember, that he has frequently made similar claims with similar justification in the past, and that they have subsequently proved mistaken. Perhaps he has overlooked the fact that he very often changes his mind in relevantly similar circumstances; therefore, on reflection, he may agree that his so-called firm resolution to give up smoking cannot properly be counted as a firm resolution in this case; it has rather to be classified as a wish, or as a hope, or as a vague ambition. It does not *follow* from the fact that he has often changed his mind in the past that he cannot properly be said to be firmly resolved now, or that he does not in this case know what he will do. The man who, on being asked the time on his watch, looks at his watch and gives an answer, may be irritated by the further question 'But are you sure?' But, if he is someone who has often in the past misread his watch, and has given the wrong answer, he will admit that it is reasonable that he should be asked to look again, to make sure that he has not on this occasion been careless once again. His claim to knowledge about the time shown on his watch did not *require* inductive support, and it was not founded upon an inductive argument; but the reasons for doubting its truth may be of an inductive kind, in the sense that the doubts are founded on the speaker's record of unreliability.

All claims to knowledge may be said to have an inductive component, in the sense that the record of reliability of the man claiming to know is relevant in assessing the justifiability of the claim. We distinguish different kinds of knowledge by the kind of support that different claims to knowledge *in any case* require, if they are to be justified claims to knowledge. But for every kind of knowledge there is the added possibility that the speaker or writer on a particular occasion has just made a careless mistake; and the best precaution against this possibility of error, available to someone else, is to examine the speaker's or writer's record of reliability in similar cases. That mere mistakes are always possible—always possible, because they often occur—is an often neglected, important feature of human knowledge: important, also, to the concept of following a rule. Because it is allowed that I may make *mere* mistakes, perhaps inexplicable mistakes, it does not follow from the fact that I have more than once deviated from a rule that I am not applying that rule. A margin of indeterminacy is allowed in my explanations of my performances. So a man may be wrong in his claim to know, although he has made all the tests and applied all the criteria. He might still just misread the results.

Another type of possible error is that of the man who has overlooked the probability that the circumstances in which he will act will be very different from the circumstances which he envisages now; perhaps he has overlooked the probability that changing circumstances will give him new reasons for acting, and for acting in a quite different way, when the time for acting comes. If he claims that he has an entirely firm resolution to do so-and-so, and that he knows that this is what he will do, he cannot at the same time intelligibly add—'But of course there is a good chance that I shall change my mind.' This is exactly what he has denied in distinguishing a firm resolution from a tentative intention, or from a vague velleity; there would be no point in using the strong form of assertion unless it excluded there being a good chance of non-fulfilment. He who states that he will do so-and-so on such-and-such a definite occasion, and who does not qualify his statement with some weakening form, such as 'I hope,' or 'Unless something happens to change my mind,' purports to give reliable information about his future. In this respect he is in the same position as the man who states without qualification that it will rain tomorrow. If he prefaces his statement with the qualifying words 'I intend,' he is in the same position as the man who prefaces his statement about tomorrow's weather with 'I believe.' He uses this form of words to indicate that he is not in the best possible position, or that he has not all the credentials that he might have, as a guide to the future. When he says that he will go by train, he is expressing his intention, in exactly the sense of 'express' in which he is expressing his belief when he says that it will rain. But by adding the words 'I intend' and 'I believe,' he may signify that his statement is to be treated (that is, relied upon) as *only* a statement of *his* intention and *his* belief. He does not claim to *know* that the future will turn out to be as he now says that it will; therefore there are reproaches to which he is immune, mistakes of which he cannot properly be accused; for the statement about his coming action, still in the future, like the statement about the coming rain, might be wrong in many different ways. It can be ill-founded and unjustified: a typical example would be the case in which a vague hope of doing something is presented in an unqualified statement 'I shall do it,' without consideration of the reasons that may lead to a change of mind, or without regard to a habit of vacillation. This kind of error would be parallel to that of the man who does not bother about the weather map, and about other relevant evidence, in telling you about tomorrow's weather. Both when I inform others about my voluntary actions tomorrow, and when I offer information about tomorrow's weather, I may prove wrong; in both cases the error may be culpable, because I did not take precautions against the kinds of error that are typical of the two cases; or I may turn out to be wrong through no fault of my own. In spite of my precautions, the facts in either case may, in exceptional circumstances, turn out not to be as I had reasonably claimed to know that they would be. Finally, an agent's statement about his future action may turn out to be not in accordance with the facts, although it was properly considered and well-founded. He did have a firm resolution, and he had considered whether there was anything in the situation that would stand in the way. An altogether surprising change in the reasonably anticipated state of affairs leads him to change his mind, or makes it impossible for him to do what he had firmly intended to do. He who had asked him for information about his future action had been misinformed, or at least had not been given correct information; but pardonably so. The speaker's error is parallel to the error of a man who had overwhelmingly strong evidence that something had occurred, and had reported accordingly; but the evidence had been a strange coincidence, and his report turns out to be mistaken, through no fault of his.

There is a close parallel between the criticisms that can be levelled against claims to knowledge of the future course of events, which are to be supported by inference from some general truth, or perhaps even a law of nature, linking observed facts with the predicted future: and, on the other side, claims to knowledge by the agent of his future voluntary actions, which are to be supported by his more or less firm determination to act as he says that he will. Both predictions and announcements of intention can be criticised for being ungrounded or careless, and they can be criticised because the speaker does not have all the credentials that he implicitly claims to have in making his statement; and they may both turn out to be unfortunate, although well-grounded in (in the one case) evidence and (in the other case) in a serious determination to act in the stated way. An error in judging the natural course of events may lead to error in an agent's statements about his future voluntary action; for he has to make some assumptions about the future course of events, and about the situations and opportunities that will confront him, if he is to form intentions, whether they are unconditional or conditional. If these assumptions turn out to be false in a relevant respect, he will have misled those who have asked him about his intentions with a view to having information about the future. He did indeed have the intentions at the time that he spoke. But his communication of them failed to serve the purpose which such communications are normally required to serve: namely, to inform others of the probable future course of events, where his future actions are the events in question.

An agent might have been asked about his intentions by someone who was only interested in him and in his state of mind, and not at all interested in knowing about the future: as a man might be asked his opinion about the probable future course of events by someone who was interested, not in the future, but in the opinion held by a man, only as revealing the workings of the man's mind. 'What *did* you intend to do?,' like 'What *did* you believe was going to happen?,' in the past tense, would normally be an inquiry of this kind. Such an inquiry might, abnormally, be pursued in the present tense; but as the whole point of a belief about the future is that it should be a true belief, so it is *part* of the point of an intention to act that the intention should be realised in action. If I am asked 'What do you intend to do?,' and if I were at all uncertain about the answer, I would normally consider *reasons* for acting in one way rather than in another; that is, I would consider the merits of the various courses of action open to me. If I am asked, 'What do you believe?,' and if I were at all uncertain about the answer, I would normally consider the evidence in support of one proposition rather than another. When an intention to act is not realised in action, this may be either a case of the agent's mind changing, or a case of events external to the agent not taking the form which was, reasonably or unreasonably, expected. If I am to know that I will come to meet you tomorrow, and if therefore I am to be in a position to inform you without qualification that I will, I must be in possession of both kinds of knowledge. In common speech it is assumed that I must, in the colloquial phrase, 'know my own mind,' because my mind will, at least in part, determine the form that this segment of the future will take. My being certain that I will do X is a good reason for an observer's belief that I will in fact do X. My thinking that I will do X does not bring it about that X will be done by me; the observer does not infer from a cause to an effect. This would be belief in magic. But my being certain that I will do X does, in the normal conditions of voluntary action and when my power to do X is unquestionable, make it certain that I will in fact do X. I must know that my mind (that is, my intention) will meet the situation expected, if the intention is unconditional. In virtue of my resolution, I know without need of evidence that, if I have the means, and nothing happens to make it impossible, I will come to meet you tomorrow. It is an essential feature of actions, performed by men, that they have a double aspect; they are normally discriminated and described as attempts to bring about a certain effect in a certain situation. Therefore my knowledge of my own future voluntary actions on specific occasions carries with it an inductive component, which is my assumption about the situation that will confront me on the occasion envisaged. Even if I am determined to do a specific thing at a specific time, irrespective of the circumstances, or even if my intention is conditional upon specific circumstances obtaining, I must still to some degree anticipate correctly the future course of events: for some normal background of circumstance is normally assumed in my practical plans. Otherwise my plans would not be practical plans, determinations of the will, but mere wishes, or ideals.

There is a now classical method of trying to separate the two components in the knowledge that a man may have of his own future conduct. Perhaps a man may properly claim to know with certainty what he will *try* to do on a certain occasion, without claiming to have any knowledge of the future course of events, external to his own mind. He will be one who knows what he wills, but does not know whether his will will be effectively realised in action. He knows what he will attempt, but he does not know what he will achieve. He does not need to study uniformities in nature in order to decide what he will, on this future occasion, try to do, if his will to act in a certain way is unconditional. 'No matter what happens, and what the situation is at the time, I shall try to break through the enemy's lines in one-hour's time': a soldier speaks: he has his orders, and he will try to carry them out whatever happens. 'Are you sure that you will not on any account change your mind?' he is asked; and he replies 'I have told you that my decision is taken, my mind made up. What more do you ask for?' But the dialogue may not be closed at this point. As we have seen, there are two more challenges that are in place, two precautions against error that we need to know that he has taken. First, a certain kind of self-knowledge is required: has he considered whether he is a man who sometimes, or often, changes his mind in comparable situations? Can he be sure, and is he justified in claiming, that his resolution is now fixed and final? This is a question to which the record of his past performance may sometimes be relevant, and relevant even for him. Secondly, and more interestingly, to what is he committing himself when he says that he will try to break through the enemy lines, no matter what happens and what the situation is? A certain background of circumstance (e.g. at least the apparent presence of the enemy) has to be assumed, if anything that he does is to be counted as a case of even trying to break through. And more than this normal background is necessary. Suppose that, when the time for action comes, he knows with certainty that there is not the smallest possibility of his breaking through: do the actions that he performs with this knowledge count as trying to break out? Perhaps they could for some purposes be so described, if appropriate qualifications were added; but this would not be the primary and natural description of what he was trying to do. He could not intelligibly be said to be trying to do, or to intend to do, something which he *knew* he had not the smallest chance of doing. His will and his intention cannot be determined independently of his knowledge of, and beliefs about, the situation that confronts him. He who says 'No matter what happens, I shall try to do so-and-so' assumes at least that he will find himself in a situation to which the action to be attempted is relevant; he must believe, reasonably or unreasonably, that his will will engage with the external world. If this assumption is not made, his will becomes a mere wish that something should be achieved by him, where the wish is a mere thought, and not a determination of the will. Alternatively, his intention may be reformulated as a conditional intention to act if some possibility of success, however small, presents itself.

There is in the literature a doctrine which does knowingly confound the will to do something with the wish that it should be done, and which thereby neatly separates a man's knowledge of his own mind, and his responsibility for his own ideals, from his knowledge of the natural course of things, for which he is not responsible. This is the doctrine of the will as transcendent; it is associated with one interpretation of Kant: it is suggested by Schopenhauer, and hinted at by Wittgenstein in the *Tractatus Logico-Philosophicus*. A man is free in virtue of his wish that it should be true of him that he has achieved such-and-such an effect. The wish is the thought that he ought ideally to act in this way. Whether it will in fact be true of him or not is another question, of which he is not necessarily in a better position, as the willing agent, to know the answer than is any scientifically competent observer. The thought, or wish, and the action, that which was actually done, lie in different domains, disconnected. The one is in the domain of the ethical, of values or ideals: the other of empirical study, of natural fact. There is the fact that a man did certain things, and that he did them deliberately and voluntarily, as far as these qualifications can be established by empirical investigation; for example, it may be a fact that he was not forced or confused at the time. But whether he acted because of his thought that he ought to become the voluntary doer of these things, because he attached value to this fact about himself, is not similarly ascertainable in the domain of fact. The 'because' here is a confusion, a superstition; his wish cannot have effects in the world. His wish, or thought, of that which ought to be, belongs to the domain of the ethical, of the private, of that which is not to be conveyed in propositions to which truth-values can be allotted. A man's relation to the world of fact, to things as they are, is either a happy or an unhappy relation, one of positive acceptance, or one of pessimism, or of indifference. One may have the story of that which has happened in the world, including the things that men have done; but the value that one attaches to what has happened is not part of the narrative. It is expressed, if at all, in the style and aesthetic form of the story-telling. Ethics and aesthetics are one, at least in the sense that arguments about truth or falsity have no grip, where ideals of life, visions of what the world ought to be like, are expressed or exhibited. There cannot be a causal relation between my thought that something ought to be done, my ideal of conduct, and that which I observably do. Events occur, and actions are performed, in accordance with, or contrary to, men's ideals: but not as the effects of these ideals.

This doctrine of the transcendent will, as 'the bearer of the ethical,' the absolute separation of what ought to be from what is the case, may be, and has been, rejected on many different counts; that it allows no coherent account to be given of our normal descriptions of intentional action: that it offers no coherent account of our anxious moral assessments of the history of our own conduct and of the conduct of others: and that it suggests a metaphysical notion of the will, without explaining the relation of the will, so conceived, to our

63

ordinarily felt and revealed desires and interests. Above all, it leaves a mystery in the situation of a man wondering what to do, and hesitating before deciding on one course rather than another; for it seems that he will have only the illusion of agency in initiating one train of events rather than another. As a conclusion of his thought, he wishes that something (e.g. that he is the benefactor of his friend at the expense of another) were true of him, and perhaps he also observes that in fact it becomes true. But his first hesitation and his anxiety had been anxiety about his *making* it true; and if he has anxieties in retrospect, they may be anxieties about his responsibility for what happened. This doctrine of the transcendent will is one more philosophical analysis that is plausible only when one assumes the standpoint of a man who is *contemplating* his own conduct and its relation to the natural course of events: or the standpoint of one who contemplates the conduct of others. In retrospect, and reviewing the record of a life from this detached standpoint, one may indeed find that there is only a choice between acceptance or regret in the face of the total history, which includes one's own decisions as equal links in the single chain of events. Schopenhauer was recommending this inactive, contemplative standpoint, this retreat into perpetual retrospect, as the only remedy for the anxieties of present activity, which on other grounds he thought must always be wasted anxieties.

If one dismisses the transcendent will, we are left with the attempts and tryings which are recorded in our ordinary speech, and embodied in action, and with the desires and interests that explain them. The knowledge that we possess, when our mind is finally made up and we are fully resolved, of what we shall try to do on a specific occasion, includes, or at least presupposes, some minimum of knowledge of what our real situation will be on that occasion. Our attempts to do X are only genuine attempts to do X, rather than, for example, attempts to make a demonstration or a gesture, if at the time of acting we suppose that there is some possibility of X being done. I cannot endow my actions with a significance, or lend them a purpose and a direction, which I know, looking at the situation before me, to exist in my mind only; this would be a kind of magic, or the play-acting of children, or a Quixotism that is already a madness.

We must conclude that the knowledge of the future, which a man has in virtue of his decisions to act, is always mixed with the more familiar kind of knowledge, the inductive kind. I do indeed know how I shall finish the sentence that I am now writing, in virtue of the decision that I have made that the sentence will finish in a certain way. But there is also the complementary knowledge that I do generally finish sentences as I had intended to finish them, and that sudden interruptions or failures are not ordinarily to be expected here. This kind of background knowledge of the normal order of things is assumed, whenever I claim to know truths about myself which are not *founded upon* induction or observation of the common order of nature. To make a comparison: I may know that I am at this moment unable to do so-and-so, and I may know this in virtue of the fact that I have just now tried to do it, and failed. This is not knowledge *founded upon* induction; but he who claims to have this knowledge must be sure that the kind of inability in question is not one which ordinarily comes and goes, and is absent at one moment and present at the next.

Similarly, I may know what I will do, subject to the proviso that nothing reasonably unforseeable happens in the world around me; and this is a proviso which does not need to be stated, because it is an entirely general condition which has to be attached to any claim to knowledge of the future of any kind. I know that this table will still be here in a few minutes' time; but I can claim certainty only subject to the proviso that nothing extraordinary is happening in the common order of nature. The admission that there is an inductive component in a man's knowledge of his future voluntary actions is an admission that applies to all those kinds of knowledge which would ordinarily be contrasted with knowledge founded upon inductive inference. One may properly claim to know various propositions about the objects visible in one's environment to be true, and such knowledge is not inductive knowledge; a man can properly claim he knows because he sees the objects before him. But an inductive inference may, in some circumstances, justify a doubt about the truth of such a statement; perhaps the speaker is often careless in making such statements, or perhaps there is some special reason to believe that he is being careless on this occasion; or perhaps there is a good reason to doubt whether his report of things seen could possibly be true, given that which is known independently about the objects in question. Everyone is familiar with the situation in which he has justifiably claimed to know, after looking, that the lost object is not in the desk, and later one is led, by respect for the laws of nature, to believe that it must have been. There is no type of knowledge of things and events which does not in this sense contain an inductive component.

The kind of knowledge that stems from decision, and not from evidence, is properly called knowledge, no less than the knowledge that I may have, or may lack, of what I want. He who waits for me to decide what I will do, because he needs to know, is no less waiting for knowledge to be imparted than he who waits for me to gather evidence about some future happening in which he is interested. But the knowledge is of a distinct kind. The peculiarity of it has sometimes been represented by the description 'non-propositional knowledge'. But this description has been found misleading. The peculiarity needs further analysis, and at this point a comparison of intending and expecting may be the relevant one.

I necessarily have at all times expectations and beliefs about the future course of events. These expectations and beliefs are correct insofar as that which I expect to happen corresponds with that which actually does happen. When I am asked, and when I ask myself, a question of the form, 'What will happen on such-and-such an occasion?,' and when I need to think before answering, my thought is directed toward that kind of correctness which is truth, that is, toward there being a correspondence, or a matching relation, between my answer and that which actually happens. My expectations may not be expressed in communication with others, and therefore no statement may be made. My reasons for expecting what I expect may also not be disclosed to others.

In the normal case a man is able, when there is occasion for it, to express in words his expectations about future happenings. There may be exceptional cases in which one might have difficulty in finding the right words to describe some future happening. An example: I may have fairly precise expectations of how the virtuoso will play the sonata, and be able during the performance to answer the question— 'Does it correspond to your expectation? Is this exactly how you expected him to play?' 'Yes, he plays it exactly as I expected him to.' Yet I might have had difficulty in finding the right words to describe the manner of performance expected. But there would be *some* description, perhaps made more specific by humming, or by less crude musical illustration, which would convey the expected performance. If I had wondered what the performance would be like, and had come to a conclusion which was correct, there must be some representation which is found to correspond with the reality. The idea that I had formed and the actual performance agree in relevant respects. When I was trying to think what the performance would be like, and to form my idea of the performance, I was trying to be in a position to *say* what the performance would be like. It is not an accidental feature of one's expectations and beliefs that they should be expressed. If I have made up my mind about what will happen, I have *eo ipso* made up my mind what to *say* about the future, if I am asked: at least I have some representation of the future to offer.

Consider now the contrasting case: my knowing what I will do on a particular occasion tomorrow. Suppose that I do not know and I need to think what I shall do. When the situation confronting me is known and clearly defined, the steps in argument by which I arrive at an answer to the question 'What shall I do?' constitute my reasons for the conclusion, which, if expressed, would be expressed in the form: 'I shall do such-and-such.' These reasons are my reasons for doing so-and-so tomorrow. They are not my reasons for preferring one account of what I shall do tomorrow as more truthful than another account. Suppose that I later criticise the reasons that led to my conclusion about what I shall do tomorrow as bad reasons; they are not bad reasons for believing something, but bad reasons for doing something. The steps in my thought that led up to the conclusion 'I will attend the meeting tomorrow' typically would include thought of my objectives, of what I want to happen, and of the likelihood of these desirable things happening, if I am present at the meeting: perhaps also a thought of my obligations in the matter. *Because* I have these interests and obligations in mind, because I have these thoughts, I come to the firm conclusion that I will come to the meeting. Perhaps I fill in a postcard to the secretary, who needs to know, and I use the third person form 'Hampshire will attend the meeting.' This is the same message about the future that he might have received on a postcard from another man, my friend. The statements on both postcards would be claims to knowledge of the future, or at least to well-supported beliefs about the future, although the knowledge or belief is of different kinds. My friend has, or ought to have, reasons for believing, or a source of knowledge, that I will attend the meeting; these reasons are the grounds, or the evidence, or the source, that he would allege in support of his statement, if the credibility of his statement were challenged. I also would have a reply to give in support of my verbally identical statement, if its credibility were challenged; I would give *you* grounds for believing my statement, although I would not give you *my* grounds, or evidence, or source, since I do not have, or require, any grounds or evidence or source. My reply to any challenge to my credibility would be an attempt to show that I had not made my statement carelessly, and without considering possible changes of mind; and I might add that there was no reason to believe that anything would happen in the external world to frustrate my will. But the reasons that I had for the conclusion, which I might also announce, not in the words, 'I shall attend tomorrow,' but 'I have decided to attend tomorrow,' are reasons of a quite different kind. For they are ammunition against a possible challenge of a different kind: not one of incredibility, but of deciding wrongly. This was the kind of mistake against which I was trying to take precautions when I was wondering whether I would attend the meeting or not. I had embarked on the inquiry with a view to having some true information about the future to give to my friend. But within the inquiry, once begun, my concern was not with what I should say, but with what I should do. In the normal case I would take it for granted that a decision about my future action will enable me to answer my friend's question; my present thought to the effect that I will do so-and-so will be a sufficient guarantee that this will happen. The fact that I believe that I will come is a good ground for believing that I will come, although it is not of course my ground for believing that I will.

Anything that I say in a declarative and statement-making form must at least pass the test of being credible. But there can be a further test, a further matter of doubt and anxiety for the speaker. Consider the following dialogue—A) 'I am ashamed of what I did.' B) 'But there is nothing to be ashamed of: it was not shameful.' A) 'I know: but that does not affect the *fact* that I am ashamed: it only shows that I am wrong to be ashamed.' Even in this particular case of announcing an attitude or feeling, A's answer approaches the absurd. If I am convinced that an attitude of mine is entirely misdirected, and that it is entirely inappropriate to its object, then I cannot just repeat that this is at the present time my attitude without being insincere, or without implying that I have a divided mind in this respect. Another report, differently qualified, of my attitude or feeling is required from me. 'It is my personal opinion that p'— 'But p has been shown to be false'— 'Perhaps it has: I was only telling you about my personal opinion.' This does not approach absurdity: it *is* absurd. Consider next: 'I have decided to do it, and quite freely decided, although I know that it is from all points of view a mistake to do it.' —This stands somewhere on the same spectrum of absurdity as the parallel cases of confessing a misguided attitude or feeling and confessing a misguided belief: certainly less absurd than confessing a misguided belief, but no less absurd than confessing a misguided attitude of shame. If I am sure that the plan declared in the words 'I shall be at the meeting tomorrow' is an utter mistake from all relevant points of view, I cannot without absurdity continue to accept this statement about my future as correct. If I did continue to assert, and claim to know, that I shall be at the meeting tomorrow, and also was prepared to say that my presence there would be an entire mistake, I would be implying that for some reason I could not help going, or that, for some reason or other, I was not free not to go; my decision would be a queer kind of forced, unconvinced decision, scarcely worthy of the name. If I am in all respects free to go, or not to go, to the meeting, as I choose, and if I am convinced that it would be a complete and unqualified mistake to go, and if I know that there is no chance of my changing my mind about this, then I know that I will not go to the meeting. In virtue of my making up my mind about the merits of the action of going, I am in a position to pronounce on the merits, the truth or credibility, of the proposition about the future; if this connection is broken, the notion of my being free to go or not to go, as I choose, becomes unintelligible.

Aristotle's account of *Akrasia* in the Nicomachaen Ethics is commonly rejected, as giving a too rational picture of human nature. But this objection misses the point, which is the precise relation, so difficult to state, between deciding that it would be a mistake to do X (having that belief or knowledge) and deciding not to do X. It seems at first sight that there cannot be a necessary connection between the two kinds of decision; on the other hand the connection between them cannot be the merely contingent one of regular concomitance. Aristotle is reluctant to admit, and finds it mysterious, that anything should count as a case of a man deliberately deciding to do something which he clearly thinks at the time, or knows, to be wholly mistaken. For what would his knowledge of mistake amount to, if the knowledge is not expressed in what he chooses, or prefers, to do? Therefore Aristotle subdivides the apparent cases of doing what one knows to be mistaken into three groups as (1) not cases of deliberately deciding, or (2) not cases of clearly knowing at the time, or (3) of not thinking the action to be *wholly* mistaken. I am suggesting that he is right to find a paradox, and a kind of contradiction, at this point. At least a man cannot be sincere in accepting the conclusion that some course of action is entirely mistaken, if he at the same time deliberately commits himself to this course of action, either immediately or as a policy for the future: and, for this reason, a man cannot without absurdity *say* of himself that he is convinced that some action would be an entire mistake, and at the same time announce that he will do exactly this entirely mistaken thing. He who offers some revelation about himself which *could* not be sincere

71

says something which is absurd, even though what he says does not contain a contradiction; the statement is absurd, because it is in conflict with the normal presuppositions and purposes of statement-making. One is sincere insofar as there is a normal and regular correspondence, or matching, between what one thinks and feels and what one overtly says and does. Insincerity is a dissociation of thought or feeling from their normal expression in utterance and in action, a willed or unwilled division of oneself. One cannot profess, or explicitly declare, insincerity without absurdity, because the behaviour is then self-defeating. My practical thought does normally determine my action and my future; this is its purpose; I will not go to the meeting just *because* I am convinced, by such-and-such considerations, that it would be a mistake to go. If, on the other hand, I was now convinced by some argument that it would be an unqualified mistake not to go to the meeting, it follows that I would now be determined to go, and I would be in a position to announce with confidence that I will go if I can. The fact that I was hesitating about whether to attend or not would count against the acceptability of the statement that I was wholly convinced that it would be an entire mistake not to attend. If I am absolutely convinced about the entire mistakenness of not going, and if I know that I will be able to go or not to go, as I choose, then I must be certain, and reasonably so, about this future contingency, namely, my coming to the meeting.

The statement 'I shall come to the meeting' has therefore a double aspect, and is subject to at least two criteria, or tests, of correctness: first, is it a reliable guide to the future, and, secondly, is the intention announced a misguided or a confused one? The speaker has normally passed from seeking correctness (in deliberation) under the second heading to ensuring correctness under the first heading; he has normally decided what he will do, with precautions against mistake in action, and then taken the further precautions necessary to ensure that others can rely on his decision. He has looked for sufficient grounds for believing that he will be able to go or not, as he chooses, and that his present decision will not be void. He has to be reasonably certain that it will be in his power to go, and that nothing will make it impossible, and that, in this familiar sense of 'free,' he will be free to go, or not, as he chooses. His primary concern in the normal case must be that the policy adopted should not be a mistaken one. His role as offering information to others about the future must normally be secondary and derivative. Admittedly, there will sometimes be occasions when it is more important that the doubt about the future should be settled, and that *some* decision should be made, and the uncertainty ended, rather than that the right decision should be made. But in general the rightness of the policy is of more concern to the agent than the reliability of the information about the future which he will soon be in a position to offer to others. The audience will accept or reject the agent's statement only by reference to the first criterion of correctness. He who thinks that my intention is a mistake does not on that account think my statement of intention a mistaken one. He would have a reason to reject my statement of intention only if he thought that I knew that my announced intention was a mistake. For what I know about the merits of the action will normally determine what I will actually do: but not, as we remarked, as cause to effect, but rather as ground to reasoned conclusion. Of the statement of intention the audience normally requires that it should be sincere and, secondly, that precautions should be taken against its being unreliable.

'If I know that I can go, or not go, as I choose, and if I know that I have every reason for going and no reason not to go, and therefore that it would be an entire mistake not to go, then I know that I shall go.' This hypothetical proposition, which relates a belief about mistake in action to a belief about the future course of events, ought surely to be regarded as mysterious, as the meeting-place of the two kinds of knowledge. How can my belief about the future be grounded upon my belief about the mistakenness of a course of action? How can I pass from a judgment of the merits of the case, from an evaluation of the practical possibilities, to a statement of fact about the future? 'I am certain that he will not be at the meeting.'—'Why?' 'Because I am certain that it would be a mistake for him to come.' The grounds for the observer's belief are incomplete, until he adds 'and he will know that it would be a mistake.' It is knowledge of the agent's knowledge of, or belief about, mistake in action that is needed as a ground for reasonably confident prediction of his action, and therefore of these future events. But I, the agent, am not in need of this reflexive knowledge of myself. If I have to come to the conclusion that something would be a mistake, I do not need to ascertain that I have come to this conclusion; I can slide into speaking about the future course of events, provided that I am sure that I have the power to act as I think best. The very same form of words that conveys to another my anticipation of the future registers the conclusion of my weighing of reasons for and against the action.

Normally I am weighing reasons for acting, and reaching practical conclusions, without imparting information about the future to others. I usually come to know what I am going to do, without needing to put my knowledge into words, either for the benefit of myself or for the benefit of others. Similarly, I normally anticipate the situations that will confront me, and the environment in which I shall be placed; and I usually do not need to put these anticipations into words for the benefit of others, or even for my own benefit. But there is still a significant difference between the relation of an expectation to its expression in words and the relation of an intention to its expression in words. If a question is raised now about the correctness of my expectations, I need to formulate them, and I may wait to match the formulated expectation with the actual events at the appropriate time. Among these expectations will be expectations about the future voluntary conduct of others. My claims to knowledge of my own future conduct —e.g. of how I shall finish the sentence which I am now writing—are not assessed as correct or incorrect by the same test of correspondence with fact. Perhaps I did know how I *was* going to finish the sentence, even though I did not in fact finish it in that way, because I was interrupted. Perhaps that was my intention, although I never in fact executed it. The wrongness of my expectation *consists* in its non-correspondence with reality: the wrongness of my intention does not *consist* in its not being executed. Even of a *statement* of intention it is not entirely correct to say that it must be wrong, just because subsequent action does not in fact correspond with the statement. If the intention is unfulfilled because some wholly unexpected change of circumstance removed the occasion for action, the statement of intention was not necessarily wrong. I had taken all the precautions against error, both in deciding what I would do and in communicating my conclusion; and, more important, it is not the whole point of an intention that it should correspond with the facts, as it is the whole point of an expectation that it should be in accord with the facts. To have some good intentions, which I do not in fact execute, may be inadequate as an approximation to virtue, as Aristotle implied. But to have good intentions is not to have nothing, or nothing of any value, even if, through culpable incompetence, I am responsible for failing to execute them.

The question that I put *to myself* as, 'What shall I do?' almost turns into, and becomes nearly identical with, the question 'What should I do?'—as the question 'What do I believe?' turns into the question 'What ought to be believed?,' for the man who asks the question; but not necessarily for his audience, if he has one. The audience may be interested in the fact that I believe so-and-so: but for me this is not a fact that I learn, except in very abnormal cases; and similarly the fact that I intend to do so-and-so is not a fact that I learn. In both cases it is normally a decision, a making up of one's mind, rather than a discovery, a discovery about one's mind. Asked for information, 'Will you come to the meeting?,' the subject does not address himself to the task of looking for the information asked for, or to the task of matching words to an independent reality, his intention; he asks himself whether he will go to the meeting or not. His policy might have been previously formed, and he might simply report it without further consideration, as he might report his long-standing belief on a theoretical issue without further review of evidence. He who puts into words, or formulates, his intention, like the man who formulates his belief, is still not in the position of the man who in his statement matches words with an independent reality. An accurate correspondence is not the only, and in the normal case it is not the principal, kind of correctness at which he must aim; he must try to be not only sincere and honest in what he says; he must try also not to be foolish and misguided in what he intends. He who declares an opinion has to be sure that the object of his belief is an appropriate object, appropriate, that is, to belief. It must not be something incredible, which a man might wish to be true, but which he cannot believe to be true without being foolish and misguided; for a man cannot have a belief which he knows, or believes, to be utterly foolish and misguided; nor can he be sincere if he reports that this is his situation. He cannot find himself saddled with a belief in the incredible, as he may find himself saddled with an appetite for the unattainable, or with a fear of the harmless. He can only find that he *was* saddled with a belief in the incredible.

If he does find himself still haunted by a thought, which he now knows to be unfounded and absurd, he still cannot say, 'I believe that someone is following me,' if he knows

76

that this haunting thought is a symptom of paranoia and has no foundation in fact. He can only say—'I cannot help thinking (imagining) that someone is following me', or 'I cannot get rid of the idea that someone is following me.' Similarly, a man cannot intend to do something that he knows for certain to be utterly futile or pointless. In considering what he believes, he necessarily has to assure himself that that which he is first inclined to believe is not incredible. In considering what he will do, he necessarily has to assure himself that that which he is first inclined to do, or to try to do, is not certainly, and beyond any possible doubt, beyond his power and pointless. Otherwise his intention will not be a serious practical intention. It may be true that Smith has a foolish and misguided belief, and that he believes certain specifiable propositions that are incredible; but this allegation about Smith implies that the allegation, if true, is not known to be true by Smith. Smith's denial of the allegation would not be counted as a relevant denial in assessing the truth of this statement about Smith; for the denial is redundant, and already presupposed. It may be alleged that Smith has a foolish and misguided fear, and is frightened of something that is not in any way dangerous or harmful. In this case Smith's denial of the statement that the object is harmless could not be counted as irrelevant, and is not redundant and is not already presupposed. He might intelligibly have admitted that he was the victim of a fear of something that he knew to be altogether harmless. He might have dissociated himself from this regrettable feeling, which occurs in his experience as does a twitching of his limbs.

The difference between these last two cases can be explained, or at least further characterised. First, it is logically possible that Smith has no fears of any kind, while it is not logically possible that he has no beliefs of any kind. It is just a fact about Smith that he has fears, and, however improbable, it is logically possible that he should be fearless. But it is not logically possible that a sane man should have no beliefs, as it is not logically possible that he should have no intentions. The only contingent matter, to be discovered, is *what* a man's beliefs are and *what* his intentions are. Secondly, the concept of fear allows that one may sometimes recognise one's state as a state of fear independently of identifying definitely the real or notional object of fear; it is impossible that one should have identified one's state, or attitude, as one of believing, and yet not have identified definitely the proposition which is believed. Thirdly, there is not an absolute requirement, built into the concept of fear, that the subject should believe that the object of his fear has that property which makes fear an appropriate attitude or feeling. He who says, 'I am frightened of X, but I must admit that X is not dangerous or harmful to me', is not necessarily insincere, and his statement may be true, as a confession of an utterly unreasonable passion. But he who allegedly has a belief, and at the same time confesses that the object of his belief is utterly inappropriate as an object of belief, cancels the statement that he has this belief; strictly speaking, he has an idea, or a fantasy, an imagination, or a feeling, or hunch, or perhaps a hope, that the proposition is true, but not an attitude that can be dignified with the name 'belief,' as this word is used, at least in our culture. We can speak of fear (and with even less reservation of a mood of anxiety) as a passion, because, and to the extent that, there is no requirement that the subject should believe that his state of mind has an appropriate object. The correctness of his thought, and the appropriateness of his state of mind, are not solely in question in his identification of the passion as being of a certain kind. A man may be frightened of a dark place, even when he admits that the dark place presents no danger. A fantasy of danger is enough. But he cannot feel remorse about something that he does not consider wrong; here the *belief* about the object (not merely a thought of some

78

kind) is decisive in the identification of his feeling as a case of remorse.

A spectrum of states of mind and attitudes, which extends from mere feeling to belief, can be plotted; indeed it has been, at least in part, by Spinoza in his account of active and passive emotions in the *Ethics*. The spectrum would extend from sensations and those blind passions, which do not require an appropriate object, to active thinking, which is constituted as such by the requirement of appropriateness in its object. To characterise a mental process as a case of rational thought is to distinguish it as an activity that satisfies a norm of order and directedness. To be counted as thought terminating in belief, the state and process must conform to *some* standard of correctness. A so-called belief, which was held in full conscious defiance of all the evidence, would scarcely count as a belief; it would be an imagination, or fantasy, or wish, or something of this kind, or possibly a kind of faith. Spinoza stressed the requirement of an appropriate object for each distinct emotion, with a view to claiming that a man who came to know that the object of his fear was not dangerous, or potentially harmful to him, *could* not any longer be frightened of that object. His state would have to be re-described. Spinoza looked for an analogy between 'He could not be frightened, if he knew that there is every reason not to be frightened' and 'He could not believe, if he knew that there is every reason not to believe.' But this analogy is, for good reasons, not a complete analogy in ordinary speech and thought. For Spinoza an emotion was a thought of an object, either a pleasant thought or a painful thought, and a thought that may be more or less disconnected and unexamined and therefore erroneous. To amend the thought is to free oneself from a passive emotion, since the emotion is identified by the subject's thought of its object, together with the pleasure or pain accompanying the thought. It is as if an emotion that occurs without any rational foundation is a mere mistake. The ideal man would have no mere feelings, but only thought-directed and appropriate feelings; he would be the responsible author of all his states and processes, in the sense in which he must be, at least to some degree, the responsible author of his beliefs. This must be too narrow a philosophy, if only because it allows no place to imagination; but this distinction between activity and passivity in the mind is the distinction with which I am concerned. There are indeed the active attitudes, to which all three of the connected conditions mentioned above apply: that they are states, or attitudes, which any conscious rational agent must sometimes have: that they are states, or attitudes, which cannot be identified as such independently of identifying a real or notional object of the state or attitude: thirdly, that the subject of the state or attitude must believe that the object that he identifies as the object is an appropriate one.

Both expectation and intention satisfy these three conditions. Any conscious rational being necessarily has expectations and intentions, and his concern in forming and stating them is necessarily with the appropriateness of their objects. He does not first recognise a state of expectancy and of intentness, and then identify their object. His unavoidable concern is continuously to review and to correct the content of his expectations and intentions, and to be sure that their objects are appropriate.

It is a truism that, in virtue of being concious, any man is always receiving information relevant to his expectations of the future; he is not only receiving it, but also actively seeking it, guided by the information which he already has. Concurrently his expectations are being verified and falsified in experience. This pre-scientific induction is the unavoidable background of his actions and of his plans of action. In this way he learns what he can and cannot do. It is easy to overlook, and difficult to exaggerate, the weight and variety of these commonplace habits of inference. Recalling these truisms, one recalls also that almost everything that a man observes is scanned and assessed for its relevance to his intentions, and, conversely, that his purposes and plans direct his attention to the information that he needs. The two kinds of knowledge intertwine, each affecting and guiding the other. But there is an order of priority, or of dependence, between them.

If my expectations of that which will happen, affecting my desires and interests, and independently of any intended action of mine, are revised, my intentions *must* be reviewed also. The question 'What will I do?' is unavoidably raised whenever my expectations of events touching upon my interests are changed; a new problem is set. I must always form my intentions relative to a concurrent expectation of what is the likely natural course of events, if the future conduct which I am now considering is left out of account. 'The likely natural course of events' here means the likely course of events as it will be, or would be, if my own possible voluntary actions in the future are left out of the account. The total course of events in the past, including my own past voluntary actions, are for me part of the given course of events, of which I must take account in forming my intentions. The situation that confronts me now, and that sets the problem, is constituted by that which has happened, together with that which is likely to happen, estimated apart from that which I might succeed in doing, if I tried. The mere fact that I now know, or believe, that something will happen in the natural course of events exposes me to the charge of letting it happen, if I could prevent it, and if I in fact do nothing. An intention to act in a certain way, if it is to be distinguished from a mere desire or hope, must be focussed upon the possibilities in the natural order of events, as the agent, rightly or wrongly, conceives them. Among a man's expectations may be included expectations of his own future states of mind, attitudes, and desires. Either by induction from his own experience, or from knowledge of some well-attested propositions of psychology, or by some combination of these two, the agent may have had good reason to expect that he would have certain feelings and desires on a specific occasion, and that he would be disposed to act in a certain way; he may be able to forecast what his emotions would be and what he would want to do. This is ordinary inductive self-knowledge, and it is knowledge of the natural course of events; a man may anticipate his own states of mind and impulses, as he may anticipate any other natural phenomena. He may learn to recognise the conditions on which their occurrence depends; they may be elements in the situation which he confronts. If he expects that he will be in a certain state of mind on the relevant occasion, and that he will want to do certain things, he has to take account of these facts or probabilities about himself, alongside the facts and probabilities of the external situation. To 'take account' of them in two ways: first, as possibly constituting reasons for acting in one way, rather than another; secondly, as possibly constituting obstructions to acting in some way in which he was disposed to act, that is, as limiting his powers. He cannot avoid asking himself the question, 'Given that the situation is likely to be such-and-such, and, as part of this situation, my given feelings and impulses are likely to be such-and-such, what shall I do?' He steps back (and the force of this metaphor will be considered later) and decides.

He must find the various paths of practical possibility in the situation before him: in both senses of 'possibility' previously discriminated. He has nothing to decide, even if he thinks he has, in respect of those things that are certain to happen in the natural course of events; and he has nothing to decide, even if he thinks he has, in respect of those things which it is not in his power to change, because he has not the means, or the opportunity, or the authority, or the skill. The agent necessarily sees a contrast between the fixed elements in the situation and the elements changeable by him; he may misjudge in any particular case; but he always tries to draw this line as realistically as he can. The range of his own thoughts and interests will determine, within the limits of the changeable, as he sees it, the narrower possibilities of action between which he chooses.

Some of his anticipations of his own passions, feelings, and desires are derived from knowledge of the conditions which generally precede, and are the occasion of, these feelings and desires. To know the causal dependencies is to know what it would be necessary to do in order to prevent such feelings and desires occurring. In general, any addition to my psychological knowledge, which enables me to calculate correctly what some of my future passions, impulses, and inclinations will be, will also add to my knowledge of what I would need to do in order to prevent these states and impulses occurring.

I may try to find the cause of, and the means of changing, those states of mind and desires which can be said to be recognised, identified, or diagnosed, as facts of consciousness, rather than to be formed as the outcome of a process of thought. The source of these states or inclinations is not to be found in my decisions; I did not make up my mind that this is my feeling about so-and-so, or that this is what I want. But for some types of states of mind, and for some instances of some types, it would be absurd, for reasons already noticed, to look for means of preventing or inducing their occurrence; and it would be particularly absurd to look for such means in conditions external to the mind. Some examples for illustration: a man who tries to induce in himself some state of calm confidence in his leader by a technique, which uses his knowledge of the bodily conditions that produce calm confidence, would scarcely think of himself, or describe himself, as having achieved calm confidence *in his leader* at the end of the exercise; the attempt would be intrinsically absurd. But it would still be less absurd than the attempt of a man to retain his belief in a proposition by concentrating his mind on the favourable evidence, and by averting his attention from the greater weight of evidence, which he *knew* to be unfavourable.

At the other extreme end of the spectrum of rationality, it would not be absurd for a man to try to control his fear of the dark by some technique, which uses his knowledge of some bodily condition on which this fear depends. Let us suppose that he already knew, or believed, that his fear was a groundless fear; he dissociated himself from it, and he would not be ready to give his reasons for having it, as he would be ready to give his reasons for some of his fears. His explanation of the existence of the fear in him would be a different kind of explanation; and, unless the explanation was a Freudian one, it would give him no place as endorsing, and as responsible for, his fear. He knows that he is the passive victim of his fear, as of a symptom of disease. Therefore he can set out to find *means* of getting rid of it; and to discover a means of getting rid of it, as also to discover a means of lessening it, would be to discover an external cause, or causal factor, external, that is, to his decision. Since the fear is not in this case constituted by a belief, e.g. the belief that the object feared is dangerous, but by a fantasy or imagination, it is not an absurd enterprise to try to prevent the fear occurring by varying the conditions that produce it. But it might be absurd in other, and no less typical, instances of fear. Suppose that I truthfully say that I am frightened of German nationalism as a political force; I would in this case normally be taken to have revealed that I believe that German nationalism is in some way dangerous, unless I add that my fear is altogether irrational. The belief is the main constitutive element in the fear, which would disappear, or at least be modified, with the disappearance of the belief. If in this case the belief were abandoned, nothing would remain that would constitute fear. The subject has his reasons for believing that

German nationalism is dangerous, and just these are his reasons for fearing it. His reasons are the precautions against error that he would cite to show that his fear is not misguided, or unfounded, and that it has an appropriate or normal object.

It is important that fear, a representative passion, can be a calm passion, in Hume's terminology, as well as a turbulent one, a considered attitude as well as an uncontrollable perturbation. I could not in this calm case think of myself as having been led, or induced, not to be frightened of German nationalism, except by a process which included my being persuaded that German nationalism is in no way dangerous. It would be absurd for me to use a technique, or to look for a means, of ridding myself of the fear of German nationalism; for I have myself formed the belief, which is the main constitutive element of my fear, and a belief is something that *can* only be abandoned by the subject as being false, or under the appearance of falsehood, as the subject sees the matter. If I thought of myself as ready to relinquish my belief under other influences than that of evidences of truth, I would not be thinking of myself as having a belief. If I now found myself discarding a so-called belief under some other influence than the appearance of falsehood, I would call in question my previous account of myself as having believed. The discarding of a belief, or the coming to doubt, that a proposition is true, is not something that I find the means of bringing about, as I might find the means of bringing it about that I should be in a calm and fearless state of mind. 'I do not want to believe': 'I cannot believe': these twin notions of will and power are sometimes applied to the pseudo-action of believing, or of accepting, a proposition. But he who cannot believe something, or who cannot bring himself to believe it, does not lack the means to believe it. I might apply my psychological knowledge to bring it about by a technique that I should be tranquil and fearless about something, previously feared, e.g. my leader's abilities, if I knew or rightly believed my fears to be groundless. I would then have arrived at an attitude which, externally regarded, would be accounted rational, in the sense of being the attitude that a rational man would have; but I have arrived by a route that is not appropriate to belief; I have got rid of a fantasy; but I have not acquired a new belief.

He who fears something that he knows to be in no way dangerous knows that his fear is misplaced; but he may continue to suffer this passive emotion, and still properly call it fear. For he continues to regard the thing as frightening, particularly when it appears before him, even though, if he were required to make a statement about it, he would admit that he knew that it was quite harmless. He will distinguish the thoughts that come into his mind, suggested by something that he sees, and the beliefs to which he is prepared to commit himself. He has no reason to be frightened; and he may look to psychology for an explanation of the incidence of fear. Similarly, a man who is infatuated with someone, and who knows that he is, may desire the presence of someone whose presence will be a source of misery, as he well knows: this also is a passive emotion, something that descends upon him, and is part of his pathology. His desire is misplaced and misguided, and he knows that it is; but it is a fact of con-sciousness which he cannot ignore. It is something given as part of the natural course of events, which he recognises, as he recognises features of his bodily condition. A certain proportion of any sane man's desires, feelings and attitudes are not of this kind; they have their appropriate objects, at least as far as the subject's own knowledge and beliefs go; he has formed them, and takes responsibility for them, and he is open to reasoning about them. When he is persuaded to change his mind, his mind will be changed.

A belief, like an intention, *must* be active in this sense. He who believes cannot at the same time suppose his belief to be misplaced and misguided. He cannot regard it as something that he happens to have, or as a fact about himself which he may deplore, but must accept. This necessity is shown in the fact that 'I believe that P' is, in its standard use, a modified assertion of P; an utterance of this form can only in exceptional circumstances be treated, or intended, as an interesting piece of autobiography. The subject may in retrospect acknowledge that his beliefs were formed, or changed, by factors other than evidences of truth. But he cannot form them, or change them, except under the impression, whether illusory or not, that the evidences of truth require the change. He may *subsequently* accept some other type of explanation of his change of opinion; but he cannot concurrently accept any other kind of explanation.

In these respects there is a distinction to be drawn between belief-impregnated states of mind, and belief-impregnated dispositions, and those that occur, and that can be identified, independently of any of the subject's beliefs. The application of new psychological knowledge in changing mental states and dispositions is for these reasons restricted: restricted, to states, attitudes and desires that are not essentially dependent for their existence upon thoughts that are properly called beliefs. I may use some knowledge that I possess of entirely non-rational factors that influence beliefs in trying to change the beliefs of another man; but I cannot be in the position of trying to change my own beliefs in this way. I must regard my own beliefs as formed in response to free inquiry; I could not otherwise count them as beliefs. So my self-controlling, or self-altering, activities are confined to the more passive states of mind, emotions, and desires: to those that are not primarily distinguished by beliefs that are constitutive of them.

I may sometimes discover that the passions, moods, and impulses, which I particularly want to prevent or to promote, depend upon conditions which I am never able, or very rarely able, to control. Whenever I discover this, I learn that these states of mind and impulses are fixed and uncontrollable elements in the situations which I confront, as are the un-alterable features of my physique and environment. Perhaps I already knew, from the experience of trying and failing, that I could not control these states and impulses at will; but I now know better why I could not. I have some explanation of why I always, or usually, or sometimes, fail to control them. and I now know what new powers I would need to acquire in order to succeed. I have more information about the limits of my powers, because I know better exactly why they are limited at this point.

In these respects there is no relevant difference between knowledge that falls into the field of physics and chemistry and knowledge that falls into the field of psychology. Whether I use concepts drawn from physics or from psychology, systematic knowledge may replace my common-sense expecta-tions of the natural order of events, which have not been corrected by systematic experiment. There is no relevant difference, in the use to which knowledge is put, between knowledge of the conditions on which a physical ability depends and knowledge of the conditions on which a change in one's own states of mind and inclinations depends. As knowledge of either of these two kinds is increased, our knowledge of the undesirable states which can be averted, and of those which cannot be averted, also increases; and concurrently knowledge of the most reliable method of avert-ing those undesirable states, which can be averted, must increase also.

Suppose that I learn that an access of fear, together with a desire to conceal myself from other people, which I suffer from time to time, is caused by a recurrent bodily condition, which, by new scientific methods, can be detected; perhaps the bodily condition is found to be regularly conjoined with moods of exactly this kind in a great variety of people. Then I know what I would need to do in order to avoid such a mood descending upon me. The case, as so far described, plainly requires that the mood can properly be said to descend upon me, or to occur. The anxiety that I feel is for me an unfortunate fact, a given element in the situation confronting me, with which I must cope. In virtue of possessing this new knowledge, I am in a new situation and with new possibilities of action before me. In any particular case, I may discover that there is nothing which I can now do to change, or to prevent, some undesirable state of mind or disposition. But it is a necessary truth that, *in general,* the more we learn of the conditions upon which our states and inclinations depend, the closer will be the correlation between our intentions and our actual achievements. The felt needs, impulses, the cravings, the moods, the sudden passions, which descend upon me, cannot be reliably anticipated, when their causes are unknown. But if their causes are understood within some systematic theory of the mind's working, and their incidence reliably predictable, new decisions are called for. Now knowing that allowing oneself to be in a certain physical state will lead to a certain mental state, one will be said to have allowed this state of mind to occur, if one could have averted it and did not. In virtue of such systematic expectations, one would have a whole range of new decisions to make, intentions to form.

Whenever I learn more about the causal sequences that are to be expected in the natural course of events, and whenever these are the kind of events that touch my interests, the questions immediately arise. 'Am I in a position to intervene in the course of events?' 'Can I get myself into a position to intervene?' 'If I can, what state of affairs shall I try to bring about?' This stepping-back to review the new possibilities is forced upon me. For once I have the new knowledge, omitting to act to prevent something, which I now know how to prevent and have the means to prevent, amounts to allowing this thing to happen. The knowledge by itself confers the responsibility upon me; having the expectation, together with having the power to alter that which would otherwise occur in the natural course of events, I am immediately exposed to the question— 'What do you intend to do about it?' Even if the newly discovered scientific explanations extended to the most intimate workings of the mind, the knowledge would still have to be put to use by an agent who decides. Suppose that I learn the causes, external to my mind, of my occasional weaknesses of will, of states of hesitation between alternative courses of action, and of my vacillations and changes of mind; these phenomena of my inner life would become something that I may try to cope with, as I would try to cope with some physical weaknesses. I necessarily distinguish myself, as the deciding agent, from the situation confronting me, which includes such features of my own personality, even of my will. This stepping-back, or 'recessiveness of I,' is built into the concepts of action and of knowledge. Some years ago, reviewing in *Mind* Gilbert Ryle's 'The Concept of Mind,' I wrote that a whole book would be needed to explain this phrase, which occurred there as the heading of a paragraph. Perhaps these lectures may do something in this direction. The two kinds of knowledge, inductive self-knowledge and the knowledge of one's present and future activities, which flows from decision, require this recessiveness, or stepping-back.

However far inductive self-knowledge is extended, the other kind of uncertainty about the future, my uncertainty about what I shall do before I have decided, will always arise. The more reliable and extensive my inductive knowledge is, including self-knowledge, the less likely I am to attempt a course of action which, unknown to me, I cannot carry through. The more I learn of the conditions on which my passions and abilities depend, the narrower the gap between that which I set myself to do, and that which I actually achieve, will become. If, for example, I know that under certain conditions I shall become weak-willed and vacillating, then I may be in a position to ensure that the worst consequences of this condition do not ensue. I may find that I cannot prevent this state of weakness, and that the sufficient conditions of its occurrence lie outside my control. I will not then struggle uselessly, as, lacking this knowledge, I might have done; but I will rather take account of the unavoidable weakness and its effects in the further plans that I make. I may try to ensure that I am never placed in the kind of situation in which the effects of this defect are particularly bad. The new knowledge has saved me from attempting something that seemed, on the basis of parallel instances in my experience, to be within my power, but that is actually not so, as careful experiment has shown. Secondly, it has directed my attention to a new feature of situations confronting me, a feature that I will now take account of.

Why then has it been thought that the growth of scientific knowledge of human nature would lead to a narrowing of the area of the free decision, and therefore of the area of individual freedom? Why has so little attention been given to the Baconian doctrine—that the more a man knows of the laws of nature, including the laws of human nature, the greater his power and his freedom of choice? The reasons are, I think, not simple. First, there is a picture of scientific knowledge, as something that may exist quite independently of the minds of the individuals who acquire and use the knowledge; the picture appears in the use of phrases like 'Perhaps there are laws, which we have not yet discovered, and which govern our so-called free decisions;' and 'Perhaps, when I hesitate about what I shall do, it is already certain, and entirely predictable, what I shall do.' These ways of speaking and of thinking may be legitimate in some contexts; but they can be misleading, if we forget that natural laws are discovered, and formulated, by men, and put to use in action as the conclusions of their inquiries; and that certainties are certainties only relative to the knowledge that someone already possesses. If I am denied scientific knowledge which other men possess, and if they know much more than I do of the causes of my states of mind, I may indeed be the victim of their manipulations, and the slave of their will. They will be able to use their knowledge to induce states of mind in me which they want me to have; in virtue of this knowledge, and of the use that they make of it, they may be better informed than I am about my future feelings, desires and conduct. If anyone wants to know what I shall do, he would do better to consult those who operate upon me rather than to ask for a statement of intention from me. This condition of comparative slavery, of one's feelings and conduct being the effects of another man's contrivance, is the reverse of the condition of the man who knows better than anyone else what he will do, just because he is the agent, and because he has made the decision. The manipulation of men's emotions and dispositions, pictured in Aldous Huxley's *Brave New World* and Orwell's *1984* is a picture of the freedom of the individual completely lost; for Huxley's and Orwell's stories represent the ordinary citizen's interests, actions, and forms of life as explicable only by reference to causes outside his own mind, causes that he does not himself recognise as the factors determining his interests and his conduct.

For these reasons an individual who acquires more systematic knowledge of the causes of states of mind, emotions, and desires, insofar as these are not the outcome of his decision, thereby becomes more free than he previously was to control and direct his own life: more free to control and direct his own life, in the sense that there will in general be a closer correlation between that which he sets himself to do and that which he actually achieves in his life. Knowledge of his intentions will be the more reliable guide to his actual future conduct.

The kind of psychological knowledge that gives systematic understanding of the causes of desires, attitudes and states of mind can be put to use, either in manipulation and control

92

of others, or in self-control, that is, in a man's contriving some technique that his states of mind and dispositions should in future be as he wants them to be. A man may on reflection want to be the kind of man who has certain interests and desires; he may cultivate certain interests in himself, and may try to smother or to divert others, in pursuit of some ideal of character. This reflexiveness—the desire not to have certain desires—is unavoidable in anyone who reflects and criticises. We do now in fact apply such fragments of psychological knowledge as we already possess in both these ways, and we could scarcely avoid doing so. But they are fragments, and the majority of what we know has been so far learned in the ordinary course of experience, and not as a conclusion of systematic psychological theory.

A man is less free, in proportion as his interests and activities are adequately explained as the effects of external causes and of conditions which he has little or no power to change, even if these causes and conditions do not include the will of others. Insofar as there are genuine possibilities open to him, and he can be said to have decided to live as he does, he can be said to be self-directed and free. Those who have defined the freedom of the individual in terms of their differing conceptions of an active mind, as Spinoza and Kant did, have made explicit one element in the ordinary connotation of the word 'free,' as it is commonly used. We ordinarily talk and act on the assumption, which we have built into the normal forms of speech, that many of our emotions and attitudes, desires and interests, were formed, and can be altered, by our own thinking about the appropriateness or inappropriateness of their objects. The distinction of desires and attitudes, which are formed as the outcome of considering the appropriateness of their objects, and which remain dependent on a conviction of appropriateness, from desires and moods that are not in this sense thought-dependent, is built into the vocabulary of emotions and attitudes. In some particular case one might have thought that a desire, emotion, or attitude of one's own would change in response to a change noticed in the relevant properties of the object, when further experience shows that it does not. The reasons that one has might turn out to be rationalisations, and the desire, emotion, or attitude might be seen to have its determining condition in conditions external to one's own beliefs. If one is convinced that one's regret, shame, discouragement, disapproval, hope, confidence, admiration, are utterly inappropriate to their objects, the state of mind must disappear, even if some lingering affect, pleasant or unpleasant, still associated with the original object, remains. Just as a belief, when once recognised by the subject to be misdirected, must, if it persists as a thought, be re-classified as a thought of another kind, so a state of mind, which in its nature requires to be to some degree founded on the properties of its object, must disappear or be reclassified, when the subject recognises that the object does not have the properties that are required. I cannot still regret that which I now know not to be regrettable.

The evidence of superficially parallel cases, encountered in ordinary experience, may in some cases turn out to have been misleading; one might discover cases in which our apparently reasoned attitudes or emotions did not vary with our changing opinions of the properties of the object; they vary only with some unsuspected external condition. But this discovery, arising from experiment and perhaps explicable within a more extensive theory of the mind's workings, still does not undermine our present explanatory scheme. We already recognise, in the rudimentary experiments of ordinary experience, that men are often deceived in supposing their attitudes and emotions to be founded on reasons, when in fact the reasons that they give are mere rationalisations and do not really explain that which they are supposed to explain. I am often brought to admit, without benefit of science and theory, that I have bestowed my fear or sadness on the first vaguely appropriate object or event that I encounter; I would have been no less frightened or sad, even if I had never encountered the object or event which I have sincerely specified as that which I am frightened of, or sad about. But there remain the more simple cases in which my fear of something, or my sadness about something, is formed and changed as I think about the properties of the object, and in which my belief that the object is dangerous, or of its saddening features, *constitutes* my fear of it, or my sadness about it.

When I truthfully say that I am sad *about* something, or that I am frightened *of* something (e.g. of German nationalism), I am not always reporting an inner perturbation, an affect, in addition to the thought of the object as an appropriate object of sadness or of fear. 'How strongly do you feel about it?' 'How deeply were you affected by it?' These questions about the intensity of feeling do require me to report the inner affect. I may myself be surprised by an excess of affect, or by the lack of it. I might say 'Of course I was sad when I heard the news: but I was surprised to find that my feelings at that moment were so faint: I only began to feel the loss intensely much later.' Language provides us with a variety of means of distinguishing a calm passion from a passion that includes as an element an inner perturbation or affect. I may truthfully say that I regret something without confessing thereby to any strong feeling; but I cannot be terrified of something without affect. When we are concerned with the effect of our actions upon the feelings of others and upon our own—and utilitarians require that this should be our sole concern—we are concerned with men's affects, or inner feelings, and with their intensities: how great was the suffering, and how intense was the pleasure, and would X be more deeply affected by the disappointment than Y?—these are the questions that primarily concern us when we are practically concerned with men's feelings. If, following G. E. Moore's prescription in *Principia Ethica*, we calculate the effect of political policies, and of all our actions in private life, on men's states of mind and emotions, we certainly will not interpret their states of mind and emotions as dispositions to behave in characteristic ways, as some philosophers have suggested. We are then concerned with the intensities of feeling accompanying the conception of the objects of the emotion as being objects of a certain kind.

We do not discriminate one state of mind or emotion from another by the mere affect, which is often one element in it. If I ask myself the question—'Was it fear or anger that I felt at that moment?,' the remembered affect is rather a symptom, as is my behaviour at the time, and the diagnosis required will place the symptoms in a wider setting. What was the occasion of this inner perturbation, as it presented itself to me at the time? What did I think of my situation at that time? Here we need to acknowledge something that has been omitted by the prevailing philosophies of logical behaviourism, and that was recognised by Spinoza: that it is the subject's *thought* of the situation as being of a certain kind which principally determines the correct classification of his state of mind or emotion. He who is frightened of something, e.g. of the dark, or of German nationalism—necessarily thinks of the object as dangerous and potentially harmful. He who is angry with someone, or about something, thinks of the person as having done some wrong or injury, and of the event as in some way constituting a wrong or injury. The objective features of the situation are not decisive in the classification, but rather the subject's conception of the situation. He who is afraid of the dark, while knowing that his fear is groundless and misplaced, is unable to rid himself of the thought that he is in danger as soon as darkness descends. He knows in his calm moments that the moving shadow on the window is that of the branch of a tree. But he also cannot rid himself of the idea, the thought, that an intruder may be lurking outside, and that the movements that he sees are the intruder's movements. In this case the fear is the thought of the danger, together with the perturbation, the disagreeable affect, associated with it. A man's anger is the thought of the wrong, or bad thing done, together with the perturbation, the disagreeable affect, associated with the thought. Just because the thought is in the normal case an element in the state of mind, together with the affect, one can intelligibly speak of being frightened of German nationalism, when the thought of danger is present, without the associated disagreeable affect. A name for that which is normally a turbulent passion can also be applied when the passion is a calm one: calm, in the sense that regret, disappointment, gratitude, discouragement, resentment, are normally calm passions, although each of them may sometimes have an affect, pleasant or unpleasant, associated with them: a pang or thrill, an access of pleasure or pain, when one is strongly affected or moved.

I dwell on the constitution of the passions, and on the elements of pleasant or unpleasant affect, and of reasoned or unreasoned thought, constituting them, because of its relevance to the distinction between the two kinds of self-knowledge. I have remarked that a man cannot dissociate himself from his beliefs, any more than he can dissociate himself from his intentions. If he self-consciously asks himself, or is asked, whether he believes that $p$ is true, he is called upon to make up his mind about the truth of $p$; for any answer to the question will count as a modified assertion of $p$. The concept of belief, as opposed to imagination and thought of other kinds (e.g. supposal and speculation), requires that a man who declares his belief in the present tense considers the merits of the proposition and does not merely report his current state of mind; and this feature of the concept is exhibited in the rule that 'I believe that $p$' is a modified form of assertion of $p$, while 'I believed that $p$ is (or was) true' is not. I make up my mind, and decide, when I formulate my beliefs. I do not observe them. But there are countless thoughts that occur to me, and that pass through, or that linger, in my mind, and of these only a small minority constitute beliefs. The beliefs are those thoughts that I endorse as true. I do not merely find them occurring or lingering: I decide in their favour. The man who is frightened of the dark may not believe that he is in danger; perhaps he knows that he is not; but at the same time he finds that the thought or idea of danger stays in his mind, and that he cannot rid himself of it. A belief is a thought from which a man cannot dissociate himself. He may say 'I know that there is no danger, but the thought of danger, absurd as it is, always returns as soon as darkness falls.' With these words he has dissociated himself publicly from the thought, or idea, that occurs to him, just as he might dissociate himself, either publicly or privately, from an emotion, or state of mind, that occurs to him. When he comes to appraise the thought, he is not prepared to endorse it; he disclaims responsibility for it. He decides against the thought, present to his mind, that he is in danger; but, in spite of the decision, he finds that the idea lingers on. In some cases of this kind he would speak of himself as imagining a danger which he at the same time knew not to exist He would not say that he thought that he was in danger, since he knew that he was not; but he would say, or at least could intelligibly say, that the thought of danger never left him, and that he could not rid himself of the thought that he might be attacked, even though he was ready to agree that this thought of his was a delusion of his imagination. Among my thoughts are my involuntary imaginings, including imaginings which I recognised at the time to be entirely unfounded, and which might still explain why I acted as I did: this thought led me to take precautions, even though I was ready to agree with anyone who said that no precautions were required. Because I could not rid myself of the thought of danger, however much I tried, I would not be happy unless I took precautions. I act in a way that is ordinarily associated with fear; but it is the thought that constitutes the fear and not the behaviour that is its consequence.

I may look for methods and techniques of ridding myself of thoughts which are painful or harmful, and which are not beliefs genuinely held by me. I may look for the conditions, perhaps conditions external to my mind, perhaps also physical conditions, upon which the persistence of these thoughts depends, just as I may look for the conditions upon which some of my desires depend, those desires which are not at all dependent upon beliefs. I may try to cure myself of my absurd fear, which I know to be inappropriate to its object, by finding the means to rid myself of the thought that there is danger; this thought is a constitutive element of the fear, and, if I can banish this recurrent thought from my mind, the fear will be overcome. Even if some unpleasant affect still recurred when darkness fell, it would not be fear, if the thought of danger was not present. The method, or technique, that I employed to rid myself of the thought that I was in danger would not amount to changing my mind about the existence of danger; for to say that I had changed my mind about the existence of danger would imply that I was now ready to deny that which I had formerly been prepared to affirm. I had not decided that a proposition, which I had previously believed to be true, was false; the change was not a case of making up my mind, or of deciding. Rather I had used some means, or method, or technique, to bring about a change in the sequence of ideas occurring in the natural course of events to my mind, just as I might have used some means to prevent or remove an impulse to behave in a certain way, which I find occurs in the natural course of events. I discover that the repudiated idea recurs in the natural course of events, as I discover that an unwanted desire recurs in the natural course of events. I am then presented with the problem: 'How can I get rid of this idea and this desire?,' where 'how' means 'By what means or method?' I used my knowledge of the cause, or of some condition positively correlated with the persistence of the idea, to produce a change in the natural course of events.

He who employs some method or technique to get rid of an idea, which he knows or believes to be false or groundless, acts upon himself, and brings about an effect in his own mind, exactly as he might bring about an effect in the mind of another. The man who changes his mind, in response to evidences of the truth of a proposition, does not act upon himself; nor does he bring about an effect. He is like the man who decides upon a course of action, who again is to be contrasted with the man who employs a technique, and uses his psychological knowledge, to overcome an inability to do something which he has decided ought to be done. He who decides to do X does not bring it about that he will do X, and neither his intention, nor the action decided upon, are the effect of his decision. The 'because' in the unusual statement 'He did X, because he had decided to X' would not represent a causal connection; for the truth of the statement is not to be established by reference to a general proposition correlating decisions to do X with actual performances of X. The statement would have to be interpreted as giving his reason for doing X—'Having once decided, I thought that I had better do it.' The agent acts on his decision and gives effect to his decisions. In a proper sense of 'cause,' in which a chairman's decision at a meeting may be the cause of a slump on the stock exchange, the chairman's decision to decide the issue before him in a certain way was not the cause of his deciding. Similarly, the man who, because of certain evidence, decides that a certain proposition is true does not bring it about that he is ready to assert that proposition; and neither his readiness to assert, nor his actual statements, are the effect of his making up his mind.

It will be objected that the distinction between a man's beliefs, and the thoughts which occur to him and to which he is not ready to commit himself, or which he is ready to repudiate, is not an absolute distinction: that there is a whole range of intermediate cases. There are cases, for instance, in which a man tries to bring himself to believe something, or when a man clings to a belief which he knows, or half knows, to be unfounded. Then there are the cases of a man having beliefs which he has never examined, and which he never would examine under any circumstances; they are genuinely his beliefs, but he does not know how, and even less why, he acquired them. There may be many shades and degrees of conscious irrationality, and of confusion, of half-belief and half-imagination. The phenomenology of belief is very various, and beliefs may exist at many different levels of explicitness and rationality. This objection is precisely like that made against the distinction between inductive anticipation and intention: between the pure cases at either end of the spectrum, there are types of cases in which a man half foresees that he will, and half intends to, behave in a certain way.

The same answer is appropriate in both cases, in defence of the distinctness of intention and of the distinctness of belief. There are many mixed, intermediate cases, of half intentions and half beliefs; but the commonplace psychological vocabulary requires adult men to distinguish their genuine beliefs from their obsessions, prejudices, assumptions, persistent imaginings, and so on; if they did not aim so to distinguish their thoughts into two bundles, those that they endorse and take responsibility for, and those that they repudiate, thinking itself would have no purpose. The distinction between 'I believe (or think) that $p$ is true,' which is a modified assertion of $p$, and the autobiographical assertion 'The thought that $p$ is true occurs to me now', or 'occurs to me under such-and-such conditions', is built into our language. I must have the means of distinguishing the thought as datum of consciousness from the thought which I am ready to assert as true. In the aeroplane the thought that it is going to crash comes to me, and perhaps I find that I cannot help thinking that it will crash. But I may dismiss the persisting thought as imagination, and not belief, since I am far from ready to commit myself to the assertion that the plane will crash. I do not think, in a strong sense of 'think', which is equivalent to 'believe,' that the plane will crash, any more than I do those things, in a strong sense of 'do,' which I find myself unintentionally doing, sometimes without having been aware that I was doing them. 'I find that I keep on thinking that the plane is about to crash, although I do not really think that it will' is parallel to 'I find that I keep on translating his words into English, although what I am trying to do, am really doing, is to translate his words into Italian.' The word 'really' may be used to mark the strong, or reinforced sense, of 'think' and 'do.'

There is a distinction, marked in common language, between activity and passivity of mind, which is applied to one's thoughts no less than to the desires, emotions, and attitudes which are differentiated by the thoughts that enter into them. I may observe, and reflect on, the sequence of my own ideas as they occur in their natural order, and I may anticipate the thoughts which will be suggested to me; I may even note their recurrences in a spirit of scientific curiosity. The pathology of thought, like the pathology of desire and emotion, is one thing, and the conclusions at which I arrive, and to which I am ready to commit myself in statements, are another. The same recessiveness of I, the same doubling of points of view, applies to 'I think . . .' as to 'I feel . . .' I may on reflection feel ashamed of feeling ashamed of X, because I may on reflection believe that the thought that I acted disgracefully, which still persists, is a delusion, a product of my imagination, a fantasy. If the affect, and the thought of disgrace, persist after I have decided that they are misplaced, then I may look for the causes of this lingering affect and of this idea, which have shown themselves to be independent of my decisions. I still, painfully, have the idea that X is shameful, and that I acted disgracefully, while knowing that these misguided thoughts are to be explained by some remote cause which remains to be discovered. Then the question arises —'Can I, or can I not, rid myself of this false shame?' Perhaps, with a more systematic understanding of its origins, I can.

*Chapter 4*

## CONCLUSION

Reviewing 'I can do it,' 'I want to do it,' and, with appalling brevity, the states of mind that are discriminated by the thought of an object, we have returned in each case to the distinction between that which I discover, and observe, about my desires and interests, emotions and thoughts, and about my actions, at a particular time, and that which, stepping back from these observed facts, I decide. It seems inconceivable that we should dispense with this distinction between two kinds of knowledge in our thinking about ourselves and our own actions; the two kinds of knowledge are mutually dependent. Knowledge of the natural order derived from observation is inconceivable without a decision to test this knowledge, even if there is only the test that constitutes a change of point of view in observation of external objects. Correspondingly, a man who knows what he is doing, or will now do, must have some knowledge of, and beliefs about, his own situation within the natural order. The proper description of his intentional actions is determined by that which he knows, or believes, about his situation.

Any facts that I may learn about the occasional capacities, desires, emotions, and beliefs of a person other than myself are facts that I need to take account of in my conduct towards him. Anything that I reliably learn about him in these respects can be called a fact, where a fact is essentially something that I need to accept as given before deciding. Equally there are facts about myself, my powers, desires and emotions, which in exactly the same manner I must take account of as elements in the situation confronting me. I discover the limits of my powers in experience, and I also find that certain impulses, desires, emotions, attitudes and thoughts occur naturally to me in the course of my experience. But my desires, emotions and attitudes do not all constitute, from my point of view, mere facts, which I must either find some means of altering, or must accept as setting unalterable limits upon my possibilities of action. Stepping back to reflect on them, as misguided or inappropriate to their object, I may decide upon my attitude to them, decide what I want to do about them and what is right or wrong about them. I may assess them as more or less appropriate to their objects, as more or less misguided or ill-founded. From the point of view of a man observing me, the self-conscious desires and attitudes that I adopt for a reason are further facts about me. From my point of view, they are not facts to be learnt, but conclusions to be reached. For the observer also, there is a difference between the fact that I *find* that I want to do so-and-so and that I find that I have such-and-such an emotion or attitude, and the fact that I have *decided* that I want to do so-and-so, and that I have decided that my attitude or feeling about so-and-so is to be so-and-so. The difference between passivity and activity of mind is not a difference that exists only relative to a point of view. On the contrary, someone who wishes to change my desires or emotions will need to know whether he must try to *persuade* me that my beliefs are false, and to *convince* me that I have decided wrongly, or whether this would be insufficient or irrelevant. When he tries to persuade me that some attitude, habitual practice, or emotion of mine is misguided, or in some way inappropriate to its object, I may in some cases agree with him, and confess that I have found by experience that I am powerless to control it. But I cannot say this about my beliefs, nor about those states of mind that are distinguished by the beliefs, as opposed to thoughts of other kinds, which enter into them, just as I cannot say this about my intentions. The fact that a man has a belief-impregnated desire, emotion or attitude, or that a certain thought occurs to him, raises for him the question of its appropriateness, or, in the case of a mere thought that something is true, of its truth. Is he ready to assert, and does he believe, the proposition that has suggested itself to him? He must make up his mind, distinguishing the mere fact that this thought has occurred to him from his endorsement of it, as constituting something that he believes to be true, or, at another extreme, as an aberration of his fancy.

To classify a thought that occurs to me as a belief is already to assess it; and to announce my belief is to commit myself to a weak normative statement. For he who says that he believes that p is true says that he believes p *is to be* believed; but he who says that he wants p to be true does not necessarily, or in all cases, assert that the truth of p is to be desired. He may dissociate himself from his desire. But his desire may be a deliberative desire, the outcome of a decision. He may want p to be true just *because* he believes that it is desirable that p should be true. This is the dividing line between the two kinds of self-knowledge: on the one side of the line, there is the claim of a man who recognises the occurrence of certain desires, emotions, states of mind, attitudes, thoughts, as constituting facts about him: on the other side of the line, he who classifies his displeasure as regret, or his thought as belief, *assesses* his affect and his thought, and claims a certain kind, and a certain degree, of correctness, and therefore of general agreement, for them. A friend who knows that I regret that p, and that I believe that p, merely knows facts about me; but for me 'Do I regret that p?' and 'Do I believe that p?' are, in the first case, partly, and in the second case wholly, normative questions. 'Is this to be regretted?' 'Is this to be believed?' call for an assessment; I have to consider the questions under the aspect of a kind of correctness, in order to be in a position to state the truth and at the same time to reveal the fact.

It is necessary to remove a misunderstanding. In stressing the role of decision, I am not, like Spinoza, depreciating the imagination, and I am not depreciating the undirected and pre-conscious workings of the mind. The most profound and fruitful discoveries of truth may present themselves to a man in an apparently unconnected manner, and without any apparent source in his own directed thinking. If one distinguishes between that which occurs in the mind, without the subject's conscious agency, and one's own directed thinking, aimed at appropriateness and with precautions against misguidedness, one is not thereby bound to underrate the imagination, as has sometimes been suggested. There may indeed be truths, and insights of many kinds, which typically are arrived at in some state of passivity of mind, and not as the conclusions of the kind of thought that conforms to a norm of logical order and directedness. As only a minority of our actions are the conclusions of deliberation, and only a minority are the outcome of considered decisions, so not all our significant beliefs and discoveries are the outcome of an ordered inquiry; nor is it a requirement of rationality that a process of deliberate decision should usually be the precursor either of action or of belief. But whatever the suggestions of the imagination, and whatever may issue from pre-conscious or unconscious processes, the final judgment on the merits of a course of action, and on the merits of an apparent discovery, is still a making up of one's mind; and even in respect of the works of imagination, which are not to be judged as conveying true or false propositions, nor as proposals of action, an artist must still self-critically make up his mind on the merits of his realised conceptions, however these were arrived at.

To distinguish between that which becomes true of me because I make up my mind, and that which becomes true of me through no decision of mine, is not to make a disputable judgment of value; and to recognise that the distinction exists is not to be committed to one particular policy among others.

Anyone who distinguishes belief from imagination must mention the norm of well-founded belief, to which all belief must approximate; just as anyone who distinguishes a person's action from the kind of behaviour which does not constitute action must mention the norm of free, deliberate, responsible action, to which all action must approximate. The freedom, which any sane man possesses, self-consciously to apply a standard of correctness or appropriateness to his own desires, states, attitudes and actions may be, in some circumstances and for some purposes, a freedom which a man might wish that he did not have. Any decision to suspend self-consciousness on a particular occasion, and not to reflect and assess, is still a decision which so far is an exercise of self-consciousness. It may open the way, in some limited circumstances and for some limited purposes, to careless responses and immediate spontaneity, which were needed or desired. Beylisme—a self-conscious pursuit of un-self-consciousness—is a possible policy, but only on the assumption that the subject is always ready to assess its effects. Language, with its first person uses of psychological concepts, leaves no option.

There remains one possible misunderstanding: I have avoided the word 'determinism,' and I have not even stated, even less tried to refute, a thesis of determinism. I have tried to specify a distinction between the observed natural course of events and a man's decisions about the natural course of events; this distinction is, or at least seems, an irreplaceable feature of our thought about ourselves, as creatures who have beliefs and intentions, and who have desires and emotions which are in part constituted by beliefs. There is at least one clear thesis of determinism that requires one to suppose that one might think of a man's behaviour in a quite different way, as conforming to a scheme held to be applicable to all natural phenomena: namely, the scheme that requires experimentally confirmed laws of reasonable simplicity which correlate, with sufficient precision and determinacy, ranges of specified inputs with ranges of specified outputs from the organism. If the discovered laws prove to be of sufficient simplicity, generality and precision, this can be a scheme of explanation that is properly called deterministic. The choice of the type of descriptions that will enter into the laws, specifying distinct inputs and outputs, is here peculiarly difficult; we are still in no position, in the present state of knowledge, to forecast, even roughly, the types of descriptions needed. But this difficulty does not by itself constitute a sufficient *a priori* objection to this scheme of explanation, as some philosophers have suggested. One would have to demonstrate that there is a contradiction, or at least an incoherence of some kind, in the requirement of descriptions which could enter into experimentally testable laws, and which at the same time can be said to 'replace,' in some acceptable sense, the established specifications of beliefs and intentions. If no such demonstration is provided, it is open to an upholder of this thesis of determinism to argue that we cling to our existing schemes of explanation only in virtue of our present ignorance. The question therefore remains: have I in the foregoing pages given any grounds from which one might infer that the thesis of determinism, so formulated, is an incoherent one? Or does the account given of features of our present scheme of explanation and description—of desires, powers, intentions and of beliefs—leave the possibility of deterministic schemes untouched?

There is a difficulty in even beginning to answer this question: namely, that one cannot reasonably claim to anticipate, or to set limits to, the types of scientific explanation that may in the future be found to yield useful results. For example, one simply does not know how successful the simulation of human conduct and performance by machines will in the long run prove to be. Nor does one know how the operations of the human brain will in the long run be understood, with what precision and with the aid of what kind of theory and model; one does not know what kind of relation, or set of relations, between physical processes and the specific higher functions of the mind, will in the long run emerge. At the present time one can only point to the *purposes* which such scientific explanations of human conduct, and of mental processes, are expected to serve, and the contrasting purposes which our deliberations about actions and attitudes now serve. No metaphysical absoluteness, or finality, need be claimed for the distinction between the usefulness of different kinds of discourse. It is sufficient that we cannot now formulate an intelligible alternative to the relation between knowing why I want X and deciding that I want X: sufficient, that is, to justify saying that we cannot conceive how one type of discourse—in particular, the scientific explanation of human conduct in accordance with the deterministic scheme—could 'replace' the other type.

This discussion constantly recurred to the peculiar features of first-person present, or future, tense statements about conduct and states of mind. It seems that these statements have an indispensable function in the thought and speech of reflective agents, who, in deciding what their state of mind and action will be, or is to be, decide what state of mind and action is appropriate to the occasion. My objection to a thesis of determinism is not that there is no possibility of replacing, in some acceptable sense, intentional verbs with state descriptions of a kind that could enter into precise and experimentally testable natural laws. This may be a valid objection; but it is not the one that I am now raising. My objection is: there is a normative element in first-person present and future tense statements about some states of mind and some types of conduct, and this normative element would not be reproduced in the descriptions which a scientific observer would use. The terminology required for deterministic explanations of human conduct and states of mind would not reproduce the relation between the first-person present and future uses of psychological verbs and the use of these verbs in the past tense, and with a reference to persons who are not identical with the speaker or writer. The shift from 'I regret this' to 'I regretted it,' and from ' I regret this' to 'He regrets it,' is a change in the kind of support that the speaker must have, if his statement is to be sustainable under challenge; the kind of knowledge, which he claims to have, is different when he is announcing what his attitude is, namely, that he considers something regrettable, from the kind of knowledge that he claims to have when he announces that he did consider something regrettable, or that someone else considers this thing regrettable. In explaining the sense, and correct use, of the verb 'regret,' one has to explain that relation between 'I regret X' and 'X is to be regretted,' which distinguishes attitudes of this type from moods, strong passions, or sensations. Such distinctions would not be preserved in a deterministic vocabulary; within such a vocabulary therefore there would be no place for discussion of present and future conduct as an expression of appropriate attitudes towards that which has happened, or is happening. More fundamentally, there would be no means of relating what a man would say of himself, in explaining, by reference to a norm of appropriateness, why he now has these desires, attitudes, and intentions, to what could he said *about* him in explaining his desires, attitudes and intentions.

For these reasons a thesis of determinism, which entails that the commonplace scheme of explanation of conduct is replaceable by a neutral vocabulary of natural law, seems to me unacceptable. But it is possible that some other thesis of determinism, which does not claim that a neutral vocabulary of natural law might 'replace' the existing vocabulary, might be untouched by the arguments of these lectures.

There is one last objection that must be met: that a persuasive definition of freedom of mind has been offered under the guise of an analysis of the use of certain mental concepts. The objector will claim that the following two inquiries must be kept apart: what precisely does a man claim to know when he claims to know what he is going to do, and what his attitude is, and what support does such a claim to knowledge require, if it is challenged? Secondly, under what conditions can a man properly be said to be free in his behaviour, and in the attitudes that he adopts? I have not held these two inquiries apart, and for the following reason. In distinguishing belief from other kinds of thought with which it might be confused, one cannot fail to mention the canons of rational belief; for a thought can be counted as a belief only in so far as it approximates to well-founded belief. So the norm of belief cannot be excluded from the analysis of the concept of belief. Similarly, an activity, or a movement, can be counted as an action imputable to a person only to the degree to which it approximates to an action, performed intentionally, with an awareness of alternative possibilities, and of the agent's own free will. The notion of freedom properly enters into the analysis of intentional action. The man who is comparatively free in his conduct of his life is active in the adoption of his own attitudes and of his own way of life; his decisions and intentions are the best guide to his future actions; and just this is the significance of calling him 'free'. He is a free man, in so far as he is the authority on his own future actions as issuing from his decisions; then his self-knowledge is predominantly of the kind that comes, not from observation and induction, but from his making up his mind what his attitudes and actions are to be.

## Chapter 5

# DETERMINISM AND PSYCHOLOGICAL EXPLANATION: A POSTSCRIPT

So prolific is the recent literature around this topic, and so various and detailed are the arguments used in it, that it may seem foolhardy to confront the issue directly once again: and in a summary form, as a postscript. But I need to write more about the familiar issue of deterministic explanation, as applied to mental states, if my suggestions about the issue in this book are to be understood and assessed. Criticisms of the first edition of *Freedom of the Individual* showed this to be necessary and showed the gaps and obscurities in my account.

I list familiar propositions which I shall take to be true without further argument here.

(a) A general thesis of determinism, applying to all events without restriction, is too general to be either falsified, or confirmed, or rendered probable, and is empty and uninteresting, until it is in some way restricted, or placed in a context within a theory.

(b) Of any given event, whether it would ordinarily be classified as a mental event or as a physical event, it always makes sense to ask what is its cause: similarly also for any specified class of events.

(c) If an answer to such a question about causes is suggested, that answer is not immune from the test of parallel negative instances, which may be looked for. This test may be more or less loosely applied in different contexts. In some contexts it may not be obvious what the implied proposition

113

is, if there is one. But even in these cases it is relevant to cite apparent parallel cases, where the alleged cause-effect correlation failed: this citation is a putative rebuttal of a causal claim, and at least casts doubt upon it, unless the apparent parallel is shown to be apparent only.

(d) Not all interesting explanations of mental events, and of the behaviour of persons, are causal explanations; other forms of explanation may be satisfactory in their appropriate contexts. But the availability of these alternative forms of explanation does not by itself preclude the possibility of normal causal explanations of the same phenomena, identified under the same descriptions.

(e) The same event, process or state in the history of a person may be correctly identified and correctly described in several different terminologies. But there is a commonplace vocabulary of mental states and processes in daily use in unprofessional talk, and in unprofessional thought, about persons' thoughts, desires, beliefs, emotions, and attitudes. This is the terminology which is used in practical dealings with people and in the ordinary planning of one's own life. It is the terminology in which history is normally written.

(f) This terminology identifies and distinguishes mental states and processes by reference both to their effects in behaviour and to their causes in stimulating conditions, and by reference to typical contemporary thoughts, which the subject may or may not reveal. The criteria of application for descriptions within this vocabulary are not strictly determined; and the terminology serves many social purposes in communication apart from the communication of information. For these principal reasons the commonplace terminology does not satisfy the normal requirements of a vocabulary used in scientific explanations.

(g) A terminology suitable for strictly scientific explanation of persons' behaviour would refer only to publicly observable and exactly specified features of behaviour, and to publicly observable and exactly specified features of stimulating conditions. This terminology would be unsuitable for many of the social purposes, and types of communication, which the commonplace terminology serves. But it could reasonably be expected to yield testable general statements which would provide fully rational backing for singular causal judgments. It could reasonably be expected to allow scientific explanations of behaviour, suitably described, explanations that are deterministic in form. There are no good *a priori* grounds for doubting that such explanations may be found.

(h) Within the commonplace vocabulary beliefs and desires are referred to in explaining most types of behaviour; and to attribute beliefs to a person entails attributing thoughts to him; and to attribute a desire to a person is to attribute at least an imagination, and in this sense to attribute a thought to him. The connections between thoughts, which ordinarily render them intelligible to us, are not the standard type of causal connection. Rather a sequence of thought is ordinarily rendered intelligible, as a sequence, by being shown to constitute a variant of some form of argument, or to be itself an argument. But it does not follow that a sequence of thoughts cannot also be explained within standard causal forms.

These are the familiar propositions that I will leave unargued; the arguments that support them are familiar in the literature.

Starting from these assumptions, I put this question: are there any peculiar features of the commonplace terminology used in the description of mental states, and particularly in accounts of desires and beliefs, which are obstacles to the standard types of causal explanation applicable to physical states? I shall suggest several reasons why this question should be answered with a qualified 'Yes'. There are peculiarities in the established, familiar descriptions of mental states, and in the ascription of beliefs and desires to persons, which are at least obstacles to adequate causal explanations of the standard scientific type, even if they do not altogether preclude them. These peculiarities arise partly from the asymmetry between self-ascription and ascription of desires and beliefs, and of states of mind generally, to others: they also arise from the form of belief statements, and of statements about desires, and of statements about thoughts of all kinds, which use *oratio obliqua* and introduce opaque contexts. These are the foundations of the obstacles to carrying through standard types of causal explanation applicable to physical states, when desires, beliefs and other thoughts are in question.

It is to be noted that these obstacles, for the existence of which I shall argue, stand in the way only when the commonplace terminology is in use. Their existence, if established, in no way implies that there cannot be found standard causal explanations of human behaviour and of human reactions which are specified in some other terminology, lacking the two features mentioned above. My argument will contain no suggestion that human beings are as a species unique in the world in not being susceptible to strictly scientific understanding to any degree or in any way. It is an argument about the actual terminology in which human beings, for a variety of different purposes, choose to talk about themselves, and in which they need to talk about themselves.

In proportion as the desire, or need, to predict and to control human behaviour prevails over other interests that human beings have in each other, a terminology adapted to precise causal judgments can be expected sometimes, and for some purposes, to replace the commonplace terminology. But such a scientific terminology, whether materialistic or not, will still encounter two limits discernible in advance: first, that a man does not predict and control every segment of his own future only by applying causal knowledge; there are some segments that he changes by deciding what he wants to happen and what his attitude will be and what he will do. The commonplace vocabulary serves this kind of thought also, when a

man considers what he wants and what he will do. His conclusion becomes a disposition or an intention. Secondly, thoughts,
and processes of thought, have their natural expression in a
type of report which is altogether unlike a report of an
observed event: in avowals like 'I believe ...', 'I want ...',
'I hope that ...', 'I am angry that ...', and 'I am embarrassed
that ...', and so on indefinitely for other propositional attitudes. In addition to these two discernible limits, there is the
fact that the commonplace terminology serves many interests
and social purposes, quite distinct from the exchange of
accurate information; and it is certain that most of these
interests and purposes will not be discarded; and, if some of
them are discarded, it is unlikely to be only an interest in
scientific accuracy and in social engineering which takes their
place.

I turn now to beliefs, desires and related states of mind
and to the way in which we now think about them and talk
about them. I will consider first the causal explanation of
beliefs.

Beliefs are customarily explained by reference to causes of
several distinct kinds: first, another belief which is such that
if it were removed, the belief to be explained would be, at
least for a time, undermined: secondly, an experience (e.g.
seeing something, hearing something) which is such that, if
it had not occurred and if all the other circumstances had been
the same, the belief would not have had the content and the
strength that it has. Thirdly, the statements, or the communi-
cative behaviour, of some person were such that, if they had
not been noticed, the belief would not have had the content
and the strength which it has. These classes, or categories, of
causes do not form a closed list; and new types of cause may be
discriminated or discovered.

The counterfactual judgments involved in the imputation
of causes of belief are vulnerable to the evidence of parallel
instances, even when the subject may be confident that he

knows directly the causes of his belief. The counterfactual judgments are ordinarily supported by, and challenged by, an immense weight of experience rather than by systematic experiment. Just as a man knows by experience the causal connections upon which his ordinary movements and physical actions depend, so he knows by experience, usually without controlled experiment, what determines his beliefs of various kinds. He learns also by experience how to change the beliefs of others by operating upon their causes. This rough, unscientific learning of causes by unanalysed experience is not anomalous and exceptional.

There is one feature of the causes of belief which is peculiar and distinctive: a person's belief, whether true or false, about the causes of his own first-order belief is normally a causal factor in sustaining or undermining that first-order belief; and this second-order belief in turn has its causes. Secondly, beliefs purport to be true beliefs; he who says to himself, or to others, that he believes a proposition thereby evaluates or assesses that proposition. If his evaluation changes, his state of mind also changes. Evaluating a belief requires one to evaluate the origin of the belief, which in turn requires one to inquire into its cause. If the cause is unrespectable, in the sense that such a cause rarely leads to true beliefs in relevantly similar cases, then the recognition of the cause and of its unrespectability will cause a change, at least temporarily, in the state of mind. Coming to know the cause, and to know more about the causes, of an existing belief is liable to change the effect.

The point can be put more strongly. One kind of conscious thought, aimed at correct conclusions and conforming to standards of rationality, is a process of testing one's beliefs to be sure that no unrespectable cause-effect relations survive in the inter-connection of one's beliefs. One tries to be sure that one would abandon this or that belief if such and such other things were demonstrated, and one tries to make the connections explicit. Such counterfactuals represent conditional intentions rather than conditional predictions, when a man is imposing a rational structure on his thought. He commits himself to abandoning his beliefs under certain conditions, even when the commitment is not a public and social act, but rather is made to himself. In the construction of an argument on a particular occasion, the successive steps of the expressed thought show in their formulation that they are taken to be the outcome of the immediately preceding steps. But it is often difficult, sometimes to the point of impossibility, to individuate the propositions that constitute the distinct steps of a rational process of thought that has led on a particular occasion to a certain conclusion. Consequently there is not the clear independence of cause and effect, at least when highly rational beliefs are concerned; and this lack of clear independence is one feature that distinguishes the cause-effect relationship in the sphere of thought from the cause-effect relation between physical states. Physical states can generally be held constant while distinct antecedent conditions are varied and the distinct effects of the variations observed. Such experimenting to discover causes is not generally possible with rational and consciously held beliefs.

This lack of clear independence of cause and effect has several consequences. First, it is difficult for an observer to make tests to ascertain the causes of a man's beliefs, unless the subject is ignorant of the varying inputs which are expected to produce varying results; the subject's own reflections on the causes and the effects will change the effects from what they would have been without these reflections. The reflections on the causes – 'Why do I believe this?' – normally leads on to the question 'Are there good reasons why I *should* believe it?', though it is not necessary that it should. Secondly, the process of reflection is indefinitely open-ended. My beliefs about the causes of my beliefs themselves have causes, and they in turn can be inquired into, and the conclusion of the inquiry may modify the second-order beliefs. Thirdly, most of the causes of any one belief that I hold are not present to my mind, and I am not aware of them, at any one time. Not only that: but my beliefs – for instance, perceptual beliefs about my immediate surroundings – are formed against a background of an immense store of knowledge and belief which helps to determine what new beliefs will emerge from the latest experience or information or argument. The latest experience or information or argument are thought of as explaining a new belief, when any question of explanation is raised. The determining background is too vast to be taken account of; and no one believes that he could bring into consciousness more than a minute proportion of the beliefs and knowledge that determine any one of the perceptual beliefs, and other kinds of belief, which he is forming all the time.

One can intelligibly speak of causes even in circumstance in which it is not possible to identify and separate all the causal factors, and all the background conditions, which would have to be mentioned in any explanation which was to be used for exact prediction and control. We do typically make causal judgments in these conditions, as J. S. Mill in his *System of Logic* and Hart and Honoré in *Causation in the Law* explained. The covering law model of causation, which might be used to define an acceptable sense of 'deterministic', is not applicable to many commonplace causal judgments, or not strictly applicable, quite apart from mental causes and causes of belief. The really distinguishing feature of the causes of belief, and of mental causes generally, is the incalculable regress of reflection by the subject who investigates his own state of mind. His changing beliefs about causes will always be modifying the effects; and this is not a transient and contingent difficulty in the way of establishing firm causal correlations. It is the essence of thinking that a person who is conscious, and able to think, should always be reviewing the sources of his beliefs, and the sources of other propositional attitudes, including under this heading also his explicit practical intentions. This reflexiveness of thought assures that a first order belief is modified by any modification of a second-order belief about it, which in turn is modified, and so on indefinitely.

I have elsewhere suggested (in 'A Kind of Materialism' in *Freedom of Mind*) that the dependence of thoughts on the subjects' evaluation of their causes can be illuminated by imagining a convinced systematic materialist. A more restricted example: suppose a person who has been convinced by evidence presented to him that his beliefs on a certain topic are changed by changes in his bodily state, and that the reasons, which he has accepted as explaining his changes of belief, are in fact largely rationalisations, and that the true causes are elsewhere. In the course of being convinced by experimental variations of the apparent physical causes of the truth of this hypothesis, his beliefs will either be changed, or they will survive as the outcome of the process of reflection to which he has submitted. The course of reflection, and the inquiry into causes, themselves become part of the causes of his belief. If there is a general law, or general correlation, confirmed by psychologists, that the changing physical inputs change beliefs on this topic, we would still need to know of each individual what his reflections on the causes of his beliefs have been, if we are to explain his beliefs adequately, or if we are even to specify what he believes correctly: at least we would need to know this, unless it was part of the effect of the physical inputs to inhibit thought altogether.

Consider a contrast with a type of thinker whose operations perhaps can be charted and explained in a deterministic style, with outcomes separately identifiable and independent of their causes: a machine thinker, which is presented with evidence, and endowed with a similarly vast stock of collateral knowledge, and then challenged with a problem. The states of the electronic circuits can in principle be charted as the machine proceeds to its solution; and an observer might tamper selectively with the circuits to test the changing effects on the solution printed out. In order to make the physical model nearer to that of which it is to be a model, we equip the physical problem-solver with a super-mechanism, which tampers with the circuits and also infers and registers the effects of the tampering. The mechanism prints out an account of the causes of its conclusions, and these conclusions are often modified by the conclusions of the internal scanning mechanism. But the machine does not function in such a way that there must be a scanner; nor does the scanner function in such a way that there must also be a scanner of the scanner. On the contrary: the addition of a scanner of the problem-solving processes of the machine, with a view to checking that the causes of the final print-out are respectable causes, is a mere addition. The instructions built into the scanner, distinguishing respectable from unrespectable causes, are structures that could have been built into the basic mechanism, with no distinction made between basic mechanism and scanner.

Secondly, the distinct states of the mechanism can be clearly stated at any time during its process of thought: there is always a clear answer to the question: how far has it gone in its thought, and what is it thinking now? In this respect there is no difference between the final state of the machine, when it prints out its solution, and any one of the transitional states, each of which are equally determinate. On the other hand the transitional states in the thinking of a human thinker are usually characterised by reference to their place in the whole process and by reference also to its outcome. A particular state is characterised as arising from such and such causes or antecedents and as leading to such and such consequences. For instance, the conclusions of my thinking usually include material drawn from certain collateral knowledge and beliefs, which I have recalled and drawn upon. But the recall and the bringing of the material into the argument are not generally dateable and separable episodes, as they are dateable and separable episodes in the functioning of the machine. A machine that is wondering whether a proposition is true or not is always at a determinate stage in its wondering; it has got so far with the problem and not further; it has passed through so many steps since it first began to wonder and it is now so many steps away from its conclusion. This is not always, or even generally, true of the mental states of a human thinker. In so far as discrete states in a process of thought are identified, they are identified and characterised by a definite place in a standard form of argument, which constitutes a model to which the whole process of thought is assimilated. Lastly, one cannot always and at every moment say exactly what proposition a human thinker is wondering about, because the different formulations of a problem, or of a solution, do not necessarily present themselves one by one for testing.

These various unmechanical, and contra-mechanical, features of thought can be summed up as amounting to a kind of indeterminacy, which is reflected in reports of processes of thought. When a person, thinking about a question, still does not know what he thinks about it, he may be told by a friend that what he thinks is so-and-so and, being told, he may agree that this is what he thinks, and even that this is what he has been thinking, though he did not admit it to himself. A man may think that he believes p, while his behaviour can only be explained by the hypothesis that he believes not-p, given that it is known that he wants z. Perhaps the confusion in his mind cannot be conveyed by any simple account of what he believes: perhaps only a reproduction of the complexity and confusion will be accurate. Similarly, in specifying the cause of a belief, in reply to the question 'What makes you believe that?', a person may mention different thoughts, including beliefs, and also experiences which explain, as he thinks, the belief in question. But he may not be sure that he has specified the various factors rightly, because he is not sure of the relevant hypothetical propositions: under what conditions would his belief turn into doubt? What are the elements in the whole system of his beliefs which might change, and which, if they changed, the belief in question would be undermined? As he tries to clear his own mind, and to answer these questions, he may correctly conclude that there is no correct answer to the questions until he has made up his mind.

When a person looks for the causes of his contemporary beliefs, and tries to reconstruct why he believes a certain proposition or theory, he is commonly seeking either to test his belief or to justify it: only very rarely would he be indulging psychological curiosity, which may be a normal motive for inquiring into causes of his past beliefs. When he picks out certain prior beliefs as explaining the contemporary belief in question, he may be said to have found his reasons for believing, in cases where the cause is a thought that could enter into a sequence that constitutes an argument, or into something that might be taken for an argument. The kind of cause that is also my reason is discovered, not invented, when I am asked the question 'why?' about my past beliefs. But my present thoughts and arguments determine my present beliefs, when they have been questioned.

The comparative indeterminacy of states of mind, and of their causes, is partly to be explained by the degree to which the subject's thinking that his mental state is such and such, and that its cause is such and such, makes it so. There are no independent tests of the truth of the subject's beliefs about his mental states, and about their explanation, other than those that arise from the explanatory role of mental states in relation to behaviour; and any change in what he thinks about present causes will by itself bring some change in what the causes actually are. Particularly where a cause is also a

124

reason, the subject's being sure that his reason for believing
p is x rather than y goes some way towards making it true
that x is his reason; his assurance under questioning that he
will, at least for a time, doubt the truth of p if x is shown to
be false, is usually as much an intention as a prediction. When
I accept the conclusion of an argument explicitly on the
strength of the argument, I am intending to reconsider the conclusion if the argument is shown to be in some respect wrong;
and his commitment to the specific argument constitutes an
explanation of the belief. The argument is no less an explanation than an occurrence or experience, picked out as the cause
of a belief, might be. The subject's conscious identification of
the argument as the factor that makes him believe, and that
explains his belief, goes some distance towards establishing
that his acceptance of the argument actually is the cause of
his belief. His belief that the argument is the explanation of
his belief is not incorrigible; he could be deceived, and there
might be convincing evidence that his reasoning covered up,
as a rationalisation, another factor that explains his belief –
e.g. for example, an emotion that would make doubt or dis-
belief unbearable. That the emotion was the cause, or principal
causal factor, might be suggested later by the subject's clinging
to his belief, without pause or uncertainty, after the sup-
porting argument has been shown to be incorrect. In many
situations the truth about the causes of a belief, and the balance
between various factors, will never be known, or even plausibly
guessed.

Alongside the indeterminacy of belief, whether occurrent
belief or dispositional, another feature must be mentioned,
which also makes deterministic explanations of belief inacces-
sible and which at least constitutes a peculiarity in the
explanation of thought. The ordinary concept of thought, as
reflected in idioms of speech, does not require that thought,
and particularly belief, should normally be conscious thought,
or should be the kind of thought of which the subject is

contemporaneously aware. That a belief should not be consciously held is as normal as that it should be conscious. Ordinary speech shows no bias in favour of conscious belief over beliefs which are pre-conscious, and below the level of awareness. To take a familiar example: he who, stumbling on the staircase, says 'I thought that there was another step' need not be implying that he had the explicit thought of another step, present to consciousness. He is implying only that his movements at the time were governed by his beliefs about his surroundings, as normally they are. Similarly, the man who is deceived by appearances and makes a false judgment of perception may explain his mistake thus: 'I thought the shadow was ...'; he does not imply that this was a conscious and explicit inference. We customarily speak as if our identifications of objects, which are often instantaneous and unhesitating, were guided by specific beliefs about objects in the environment, and from these beliefs we infer our conclusions. These are usually not conscious inferences, even though we may later say 'I thought the so-and-so was a so-and-so, and that is where I was wrong'. We may remember what the perceptual clues were that led to a perceptual belief without our having explicitly thought about them at the time. Alternatively we may not remember, and we may infer what our inferences must have been, given the situation and the probable inputs of information.

Just as we ordinarily talk of inferences which are not conscious inferences at the time, and which are not inferences of which we were aware, so we talk of collateral knowledge, beliefs, suppositions and assumptions which are all the time having their effects on behaviour. The connections between the thoughts and the behaviour are usually inferred and distinguished with difficulty. For this reason, and apart from the previously mentioned difficulties of indeterminacy, the way in which we explain beliefs is very unlike the standard methods of scientific explanation. If a psychologist experiments upon a subject to determine how a specific range of his perceptual beliefs are formed – for example, his judgments of distance – he will find that certain types of perceptual clue lead to certain responses in judgments of distance. If he wished to press for further explanations as to how this type of clue led to this type of judgment, he might turn away to investigate the physiological mechanisms involved: the operations of the brain and how they could be disturbed or interrupted by physical and chemical operations. It would be difficult to look for further explanations at the mental level. Part of the difficulty would be that the immense store of collateral knowledge involved in the inferences made would not be present to the mind of the subject and would not easily be discriminated and reported by him. He would not know what all the separate steps in his own inferences were: and he could only try to learn, as an observer might learn, by comparing the inferences made by different subjects who had had different information and experiences in a different personal history. The inquiry would be of baffling complexity; there would be too many independent variables for definite conclusions to be drawn. Not only that, but the term 'perceptual clue' conceals the fact that a man may see or notice things and features which he does not know, or is not aware, that he has noticed; and he may instantly form beliefs which lead to other beliefs, without his being aware of this chain of consequences.

Three separate reasons have so far been given for saying why the causal explanation of beliefs is not ordinarily a deterministic explanation: (1) that the subject's beliefs about the explanation of his own beliefs in part, though only in part, determine what these first-order beliefs are: and so also for second-order beliefs: and so indefinitely for higher orders. Therefore a person's beliefs are not independent of his reflections upon them, which modify them. (2) An experimental inquiry into the causes of a person's beliefs meets the difficulty that the subject will evaluate his changing states of mind by reference to their causes; and what he believes, the precise content of his beliefs, is not independent of the causes that led him, as he believes, to his conclusions. It is an implication of (1) and (2) that a person's state of mind in respect of some belief may at some specific time be indeterminate, in the sense that no clear and definite account of it is true, and that the only true account is one that shows contradiction and confusion, because the subject's mind is not made up; (3) The thoughts of a person, and particularly his beliefs, are determined by other thoughts, most of which are below the level of consciousness; they are thoughts of which he is not explicitly aware, and they form a vast network of stored collateral knowledge and belief. This is a feature of the ordinary concept of thought and of belief; it is presumed that at all times much is going on in the mind of a person of which he is not contemporaneously aware, until questions are asked and he is prompted to bring into consciousness the inferences that he is constantly making at all times when he is awake.

For these reasons the explanation of beliefs, within the commonplace terminology, is very unlike the explanation of states of a machine; and a machine is the paradigm of a deterministic system, just because (a) its successive states can be clearly and definitely, and in principle exhaustively, stated, and these states are always distinct; (b) there is no problem of indeterminacy; the states are independent of the observer; (c) the states can be experimentally varied one by one, and the independent outcome observed, and definite universal correlations established. The singular counterfactual judgments implied by explanations of beliefs do not have the backing of similarly well confirmed general statements. Rather they are loose explanations for some of the same reasons that the typical judgments of a historian about the causes of a war, and about the might-have-beens of history, are loose. In both cases the looseness is contrasted with the strictness and reliability of the counterfactual judgments which an applied science requires. This is not to deny that some judgments about the causes of a belief are known with certainty to be true, just as some judgments about causes of change in political or economic history are known with certainty to be true.

If this conclusion about causes is valid for belief, it is valid for the whole range of propositional attitudes: for the same three features, just mentioned, are common to all propositional attitudes: 'I am disappointed that so-and-so has happened', 'pleased that', 'sad that', 'I wish that so-and-so would happen', 'I am frightened that', 'angry that', and so on. There is an indefinite range of intentional states which have a proposition in the place of an object of the verb and which have a verb representing an attitude or sentiment. In every case the subject's belief about the nature of his attitude or sentiment, and also his belief about its cause, in part determine what his attitude or sentiment actually is. A man's attitudes and sentiments are modified by his beliefs and doubts about their causes. Secondly, the subject evaluates his attitudes and sentiments by reference to their causes, using some standard of the appropriateness or the reasonableness or the desirability of his having this attitude or this sentiment for this reason. He may wish that he did not wish for the things that he does wish for, and be ashamed that he is ashamed of certain things; and he may not only defend, but also explain these second-order attitudes and sentiments by referring to their causes. The indefinite reflexiveness of thought enters into propositional attitudes, and also into the less headstrong or passionate or thoughtless sentiments. Thirdly, all propositional attitudes and sentiments, not only beliefs, have causes in other attitudes and sentiments and beliefs which are not always, or even usually, conscious ones. Propositional attitudes and sentiments involve thoughts of an object, not all of which are conscious thoughts. A person is explicitly aware at any

129

time of only a few of the attitudes and sentiments that could be correctly attributed to him. An attitude or sentiment may be truly imputed to a person on the evidence of a clear pattern of otherwise inexplicable behaviour which can best be explained by a particular attitude or sentiment; either an observer or the subject may infer the attitude or sentiment. The subject is in the best position to judge what his attitude or sentiment is or was; for the subject usually knows directly and without inference what he was thinking at the time, and therefore can know whether the content of his thoughts was such as to exclude the sentiment imputed.

All that has been said of attitudes and sentiments applies also to desires, or at least to those desires that are intentional states and that involve the thought of an object of desire. It is perhaps arguable that there are entirely unthinking desires, or lusts, such as the desire for drink when dehydrated, which are not properly to be counted as mental states. One needs to distinguish the physical sensations that accompany the desire to eat and to drink when one is hungry or thirsty from the desire itself. Ordinarily desires explain actions, when taken in conjunction with beliefs; the three form a tripod for inter- pretation. Given knowledge of any two points on the tripod, the third can be plausibly inferred. If we know what a man did, and if we know what he believes or knows about the situation in which he is placed, we can infer what he wants to have or to achieve. Similarly, if we know what a man believes about his situation and what the system of his wants and interests are, we can plausibly infer what he is doing, or what he will do. The tripod permits a characteristic looseness, and on occasions an incurable uncertainty, in explanation. We can argue that a man's beliefs cannot be what they appear to be, or that his desires cannot be what he supposed that they were, or that his intentions in action cannot be what they seemed, until we arrive at a standard and acceptable overall account of the man. The explanation may be loose, in the sense that the standard and acceptable account is not prescribed by any exact quotable rule; nor is there a definite list of acceptable standard relations between types of belief, types of desire and types of action. Secondly, neither the set of a man's beliefs at any given time, nor the set of his desires at that time, are ordered sets of distinct elements. We speak of different formulations of the same belief, and of specific beliefs on specific topics being modified and changed. Yet we are not ready with a uniform way of individuating beliefs or a clear way of distinguishing them. Nor are we ready with a principle of individuation which would enable one to separate desires clearly from each other, and then to produce a map of a man's desires, showing the dependence of one on another. It is the same difficulty that makes such a map or diagram, showing the causal interrelations of a man's beliefs, virtually impossible: the formulation of the desires, and the specification of the objects of desire, will require either that the exact words of the subject are used, when they are available, or more or less arbitrary specifications of the desires in another terminology: and the exact words of the subject, even when they are available, may embody a number of misconceptions and confusions in the subject's mind. Thirdly, desires are in conflict and desires override each other; and it is intrinsic to them that they should, which is not true of beliefs. The map of a man's desires, like the map of his beliefs, would show dependences of one desire on another; but it would also show intersections representing points of conflict. Both maps could be composed only with very arbitrary assumptions about the individuation of desires and great simplifications of the thoughts constituting the beliefs and desires. Also the map would need to show the constant process of interaction and modification of beliefs and desires, as new information is received and as previous thoughts are made the objects of reflection and are thereby modified.

In addition to the sources of indeterminancy already mentioned, desires are liable to be ambivalent in several different ways. One may be both attracted towards something, for example, a future event, and want it to happen, and at the same time also fear the event and want to avoid it; also the event may be attractive in some respects, and in virtue of some characteristics, and repugnant in some respects, and in virtue of some characteristics. These complexities are intrinsic to the concept of desire. Contradictory beliefs are of course commonly held by the same person at the same time. But it is not absurd to imagine someone who has continually tried to eliminate contradiction, at least from his standing beliefs, and who has largely succeeded. Such a rational man would perhaps not be an inhuman monster. But a man who was never involved either in conflict of desire or in ambivalence would be inhuman and is scarcely imaginable.

From all these considerations one may conclude that both a man's beliefs, and even more his desires, are often not clearly identifiable at specified times, and therefore that they are ill-suited to deterministic explanations; and this is true even apart from the fact that knowledge of the cause of beliefs and desires is apt on many occasions to modify the effect. The defects of the psychological vocabulary, from the point of view of deterministic explanation, are not be eliminated without frustrating the purposes that the vocabulary serves. The looseness and indeterminacy of the vocabulary are not to be cured, if only because a man who asks himself why he wants something, or why he believes something, is usually not looking for a cause that is clearly distinct from the effect in the way in which a cut is clearly distinct from the pain that it causes. The vocabulary of beliefs, desires, attitudes, and sentiments differs from the physical vocabulary in that the former does not in general specify distinct states which can be pinpointed as discrete states of the organism at a particular time. A process of thought is not a sequence of clockable discrete states of the organism, as a physical process in the organism is, or as even a succession of sensations is. Suppose that for the purposes of some medical research it became necessary to distinguish separate sensations experienced in a sequence of sensations; then a somewhat arbitrary and *ad hoc* convention could be introduced, perhaps picking out changes in quality of sensation as marking borderlines between different sensations; differences of location might also be used. If it seemed similarly necessary to individuate thoughts in a sequence of thought, the obvious method would be to take as distinct thoughts distinct sentences in the natural expression of the thoughts. But this would make the sequence of thoughts relative to a particular language, and relative to a particular choice of syntax within that language.

What is the need for deterministic explanations? They are the type of explanation that one needs for a reliable method of control and manipulation: briefly, for a technology. If, for instance, one is trying to control pain, one needs to know the mechanism at work, and therefore to know the general laws that correlate inputs to the nervous system, and to the brain, with the resulting sensation. If this information is available, one has a path to a technology of anaesthesia, on which one can rely. There is a comparatively minor difficulty in finding experimentally an exact and general law that correlates physical stimuli with a sensation of pain; the effect is not immediately measurable in quantitative terms, and exactness is therefore not easily achieved. But the technology that can modify and control sensations does not meet difficulties which are so fundamental that one may doubt whether it is a technology at all, in the sense that surgery is a technology. It is true that the anaesthetist cannot directly see the desired effect of his operations, as the surgeon can; and he cannot point directly to the desired effects for the benefit of his students, as the surgeon can. He can see, and he can point to, some effects, namely, the patient's tranquil or sleepy behaviour: but the important desired effect is the absence of pain, and that is not something that is visible to any observer, as the absence of a limb is. The technology may therefore be more difficult to establish.

The idea of a technology that would control beliefs, desires, and other intentional states by applying knowledge of the mechanisms on which they depend is not a clear idea: it is not clear, in proportion as the intentional state cannot be assimilated in at least one relevant respect to a sensation. Consider a case that may be near to a borderline between an intentional state and a sensation. A man has a desire, amounting to a craving, which he for good reasons wishes he did not have. He acquires a technique for getting rid of the desire as soon as he feels its onset. Perhaps the technique is a form of aversion therapy which involves various operations that a man can perform upon himself as well as upon another. If the technique required a more or less systematic knowledge of the stimulating conditions and of the state of the nervous system, which together caused the onset of the desire, then the technique would amount to a technology. If the mechanism was understood systematically and with some exactness, then a variety of willed adjustments to desires and aversions falling within the same range would be possible. Suppose that the first-order desire was for something concrete and physical, e.g. alcohol; then there might be a second desire to get rid of the desire for good reasons, because other desires were being frustrated by alcoholism. This second-order desire might reasonably be satisfied by a technique, analogous to the techniques of anaesthesia and surgery. The first desired state was a state of consciousness, the effect of alcohol, and the desire was not itself the outcome of much calculation or thought. The part that thought may play in the formation of the first order desire, the thought either of some particular alcoholic drink or just of some alcoholic drink, may in such a case be very small. Just because the thought involved may be minimal and therefore may be neglected, the desire may be assimilated to a sensation and one may naturally speak of 'feeling' its onset, as one feels the onset of an ache or pain. The assimilation of a desire to a sensation depends on the comparatively minor part of thought in the specification of the desire.

Consider for contrast a man who has at intervals a craving, or at least an intense desire, to dress in women's clothes, and who at the same time wishes that he did not have this desire, because its gratification is apt to cause the frustration of his other desires. The first-order desire cannot be assimilated to a sensation, because the thought of the clothes, and of himself as being temporarily like a woman, or the imagination of himself as a woman, is essential to the desire. The thought of femininity makes this particular desire what it is and distinguishes it from other desires which might manifest themselves in the same behaviour, where 'same' refers to what the external observer sees. The thought that informs the very specific desire of a transvestite need not be articulated and explicit in the mind of the subject. It need not even be fully conscious. There are cases in which a child has this desire, and becomes aware of an overwhelming impulse to dress in his mother's clothes, without his knowing why he has this desire; this may even happen without his knowing what the desire is, in the sense of knowing how the desire is to be most accurately characterised. The desire to wear women's clothes, with the attendant thought of their femininity, is quite different from the desire to wear one's mother's clothes, with the attendant thought that she is one's mother. Femininity is not the same as maternity, and what is wanted is different, even if in the particular circumstances the desire is focussed upon the same objects.

An accurate characterisation of the desire will mention the thought that enters into the desire, including the thought of the reason for the desire or of the feature that makes the object desired desirable. The cases of sexual perversions, and of fetishisms and of allied aberrant states, are interesting in this connection because they show thought constituting distinct desires, which are thought-impregnated, but often at a very inarticulate and inexplicit level. It is a peculiarity of desires of this type that they may be very strong, and that the subjects may speak of them as compulsions and even as being irresistible. It is also characteristic of such desires that the subjects are often surprised by them and are often at a loss to explain them. The often complex thoughts, and associations of ideas, which enter into such desires are typically not fully conscious thoughts, of which the subject could give a clear account. The thought that is the content of his desire, and that picks out an object, might be very specific, and yet he may be unable to say why he has this thought and what its source is. He only realises that he has the thought through feeling the desire.

In such cases it would be natural to look for an explanation of the desire in the fantasies and in the unconscious thought of the subject, as these are revealed in other ways and on other occasions. One certainly would not expect to find, as one might with the craving for alcohol, the precise initial conditions which need to be varied if the desire is to be controlled, and which adequately explain the desire. As the desire is so described as to be naturally explained by the thought that enters into it, the control of it also seems to call for knowledge of the subject's thought; and this entails his making his less than conscious thoughts explicit and his testing them against his other desires and beliefs. This need not always be difficult. The recognition of a desire, not previously conscious, may often be immediate and effortless, while on other occasions it may require an effort of thought and the overcoming of difficulty in making out what exactly is wanted.

The deterministic scheme, with the accompanying idea of a possible technology, does not fit well with the alteration of desire by the subject's reflection. At first look at least, there seem to be two contrasting ways of explaining a desire, leading to two contrasting ways in which a person may try to control and to change his own desires. But the traditional scheme, which distinguishes the lusts from thoughtful desires, may turn out to be much too simple, and to reflect too grossly simple moral ideas. Any study of sexuality shows that thought, usually in the form of fantasy, enters into a great variety of sexual desires, which are normally also associated with physical causes. The traditional equation of physical desire, or lust, with unthinking desire is not warranted by the evidence. Nor is it true that the more reflective and fully conscious desires, which are in this sense rational, are necessarily or always the most complex. On the contrary, there can be pre-conscious and unconscious desires which are shown to have developed from very complex processes of unreflective and imaginative thought.

Just as there is no general method of enumerating, or of setting a limit on, the store of collateral knowledge, and of collateral beliefs, called into play on a certain topic, e.g. in identifying some perceived object: so also there is no way of enumerating, or of setting a limit on, the set of desires and interests that may be called into play by a situation calling for action. Sometimes the subject's behaviour may be clearly and simply explained by a few clearly distinguishable and countable desires which, taken in conjunction with a few clearly statable beliefs, lead to an obvious outcome. Then the ancient analogy between desires and lines of force, the analogy of psychological mechanism, is entirely natural: in such cases unavoidable. But the analogy can only be sustained, and extended to less straightforward cases, bv overlooking the tangles of intentionality, already mentioned, which make the individuation of desires problematical, and also the peculiarities of desires among propositional attitudes, peculiarities that compound the problem of individuation: that desires may be ambivalent, that there is a difference between two desires that are in conflict and two co-existing desires which cannot both be satisfied: that one desire may override another: that there is no clear way of distinguishing between a desire that is over-ridden by another desire and a desire that changes its object. The mechanical analogy, when pressed, cannot be taken seriously, even though it is entirely natural that psychological explanation should be modelled to some degree on physical explanation. There are too many independent reasons for insisting on the ineliminable indeterminacy of psychological explanations when compared with explanations of physical states and processes.

Belief and desire are the two propositional attitudes that are essential to explanations of conduct, both from the standpoint of an observer explaining the conduct of another and from the standpoint of an agent reviewing the reasons that he has for acting in one way rather than another. The indefinitely open range of other propositional attitudes – fear that, pleased that, embarrased that, angry that, ashamed that, disappointed that, hoping that, mortified that, anxious that, regretting that, and so on – each always involve a belief or imagination that so-and-so is the case, together with a disposiion or desire to behave in some broadly characterisable manner in some broadly characterisable circumstances, actual or notional. For present purposes there is no need to show the same looseness in contexts of explanation, the same indeterminacy in statements that attribute these states of mind to persons, for each of these sentiments. As they all involve thought of an object characterised in some way, they are all subject to the same scheme of explanation, with its distinguishing features: that the subject's belief, and change of belief, about the correct account of his own state of mind, and about the explanation of it, always modifies the state of mind: that the thought constituting the state of mind is causally linked to a vast background of beliefs and imaginations, of which only a few are brought to consciousness and to attention at any one time: that reflection on the causes of a thought and of an associated disposition is at the same time usually an assessment of them as appro-

138

priate or not, or as wrong or undesirable; and this reflective criticism confuses explanation with justification in the mind of the subject, who is generally in the best position to judge what his state of mind is, because he can be expected to know what he is or was thinking. In so far as he is confused, and in so far as his thought is continuing and has not reached a conclusion, there will be no determinate answer to a Yes-or-No question about his contemporary state of mind.

'I do want it in one way and in another way I do not': 'I oscillate between loving and hating him': 'I am half attracted, half repelled': 'Perhaps I am rather frightened of it': 'I am not sure whether I am pleased that it has happened or not': 'I am half ashamed of it, half pleased'. A divided mind is not abnormal or unexpected, and no refinement of the psychological vocabulary will alter this, nor prevent uncertainty and consequent confusion of mind; for the reasons given, these are intrinsic features of thought and of mental processes generally.

Deterministic explanation exhibits a universal correlation between more or less exactly stated initial conditions and more or less exactly stated outcomes, with the assumed background conditions also statable: a law-like formulation which is also part of a theory. The physical machinery of brain and sense-organs, on which thought and knowledge depend, operate in accordance with this deterministic scheme, even if physicists impute some degree of indeterminacy to some smaller physical systems. The physical actions and motions of a person, including those that go with his talking and his listening, are instances of law-like patterns which we presume will be explained in chemistry and in other relevant sciences. 'We presume' is added, as a note of caution, because there is no *a priori* certainty that anticipations, based on the physical sciences in their present state, will in fact be entirely realised by future developments in knowledge, e.g. in physiology and biology. However difficult it may turn out to be to discover, and to represent, the workings of the brain, and the mechanisms of thought, we shall continue to develop the available physical and chemical theory of the day in the hope of understanding. The terms 'mechanism' and 'machinery' may come to seem rather inappropriate, because the machinery may turn out to be very unlike the machines that are at present known and that can at present be imagined. The machinery may even turn out to be so complex that our theories fall short of being adequate representations, and we may despair of ever reaching a full understanding of how the organism performs its higher functions: e.g. how the brain operates in composing sentences and in interpreting the sentences that are heard. We cannot reasonably anticipate the rate of progress of the relevant sciences or the forms that they will assume as they advance. For instance, it is possible that the uncertainty, which is a principle in physical theory, will have further and now unexpected applications within the theories that give an acceptable representation of some human performances, or of biological systems generally. If this were to happen, then the word 'deterministic', used in this discussion, will be out of place. But it will still be true that the scheme of explanation for bodily, and therefore for physical, processes will need a vocabulary that allows for comparatively clear and definite identification of the elements in the explanation, and one that is comparatively exact; and it will need a vocabulary that is applied by all observers and experimenters from a single and constant standpoint. The vocabulary used to communicate thoughts will always be applied from two different standpoints: that of a person thinking and that of a person reporting or inferring the thoughts of another or of his own past. The vocabulary applied to psychological states is a vocabulary adapted, in the conditions of its application, to two different purposes in two different types of situation: that of a man making up his mind what he believes, wants, fears and so forth: and that of a man recording what he has believed and wanted and what is believed and wanted by another person. The reflexiveness of thought entails a shifting of standpoint, because one considers what one has believed and wanted, and asks oneself why; and this reflexiveness in turn entails the kinds of indeterminacy already discussed, particularly the indeterminacy that results from changing second-order thoughts about the causes of thoughts.

The conclusion that I draw from these considerations is not a new or unfamiliar one. Human beings can be considered as very complex organisms which function in accordance with the laws of physics and of chemistry, as do all other biological systems. Among the complex powers built into the physical mechanisms is the power to speak and to understand a language, which entails that the behaviour of the organism is to be explained, not only by the actual situations in which it is placed together with its known needs and appetites, but also by spoken beliefs about its situation, and by beliefs about its own needs and appetites, and by beliefs about a remote future. All and only creatures who have a language have beliefs about the remote future, which help to explain what they do. This power to speak a language once developed, multiplies itself, like a cancer, and the power to have thoughts about thoughts develops from it. A speechless creature acquires through its sense organs unspoken expectations and beliefs about its present situation and the immediate future following it. These beliefs, together with unspoken desires and needs, determine and explain most of its behaviour. These expectations and beliefs are the direct effects of external things acting on the creatures through sense-organs and brain. Therefore we can imagine a physical model of the input signals from the environment setting in motion the already adjusted machinery of the brain, which then leads to an outcome either in behaviour, including speech, or in a re-adjusted brain state, or in both. The imagination may in the future turn out to be vain, in the sense that we in fact are not able to develop the model satisfactorily, or to exhibit a realisation of it. The physical complexities may be too great and our powers of mind may be insufficient, or for many years they may appear to be so. But we shall certainly persevere in the attempt, and we shall use such fragments of adequate knowledge that we do acquire in a new technology: to improve our thinking and mental health and efficiency generally, as we now use knowledge of the mechanisms of eye and ear to assist sight and hearing.

One may say that the sense of freedom that men undoubtedly have is to be identified with their power of reflection and with the self-modifying power of thought. The intuition that when we are thinking of ourselves as thinking beings, we are excluding deterministic explanations of our performances, can be justified, so far at least.

The conclusion is near to Spinoza's. The relation between thought and the physico-chemical mechanisms of the body and brain is still left unclear.

Anomalous monism

Idea (truth & prob)

self-reference as

source of mind-awareness

& self-consciousness ?

only

Is it same →

No causal

interaction

T — mind-mental

P — body /
extended
world ?
physical